Biblical Discipleship

By Bob Warren

Editor, Jhonda Johnston
Special thanks to Sam Perry for support on the maps
Cover Design, Brent Armstrong and Jenelle Schimpf

ISBN 9781627270601

To my faithful brother, Larry Heppes,
who discipled me and taught me the
importance of sitting at the feet of Jesus.

Table of Contents

Outline

Section I: About Discipleship

    A. The Importance of Discipleship

    B. The Definition of a Disciple

    C. The Life of Freedom Experienced by the Disciple

    D. The Importance of Learning To Sit with Christ

    E. Learning To Sit with Christ

Section II: The Life of Moses

    A. Moses' Early Life (First 40 Years)

    B. How Moses Became a Disciple (Second 40 Years)

    C. Moses' Life as a Disciple (Last 40 Years)

        1. How Moses Led Israel

        2. How Moses Discipled Joshua

Section III: The Life of Paul

    A. Paul's Early Life

    B. What Helped Prepare Paul for Salvation

    C. Paul's Salvation Experience

    D. How Paul Became a Disciple

        1. Paul's Time in Damascus (Acts 9:8-22)

        2. Paul's Time in Arabia (Acts 9:23a, Galatians 1:11-17)

        3. Paul's Time in Damascus (Acts 9:23-25, Galatians 1:17b)

        4. Paul's Time in Jerusalem (Acts 9:26-29)

        5. Paul's Time in Tarsus (Acts 9:30-31)

6. Paul's Time in Antioch (Acts 11:19-26)

7. Paul's Time in Jerusalem (Acts 11:27-30, Acts 12:1-25)

E. Paul's Life as a Disciple

1. Paul's First Missionary Journey and First Convert (Acts 13-14)

2. Paul's Trip to Jerusalem (Acts 15:1-29)

3. Paul's Return to Antioch (Acts 15:30-35)

4. Paul's Second Missionary Journey (Acts 15:36-18:22)

5. Paul's Third Missionary Journey (Acts 18:23-21:14)

6. Paul's Time in Jerusalem (Acts 21:15-23:30)

7. Paul's Time in Caesarea (Acts 23:31-26:32)

8. Paul's Trip to Rome (Acts 27:1-28:31)

F. How Paul Discipled Timothy

1. What Attracted Timothy to Paul

2. How Paul Taught Timothy

3. What Paul Taught Timothy

4. Paul's Instruction to A Mature Timothy

Section IV: Learning to Share your Testimony

A. Paul's Testimony

B. Application Weeks (Sharing Your Testimony),

The Master Plan of Evangelism and *Ordering your Private World*

C. Why You Can Share your Testimony without Fear

Introduction

This course has been written for those who desire intimacy with Jesus Christ—who want to know Him as their life (Philippians 3:10; Colossians 3:4). Our goal is not to learn the Bible as an end in itself, or to learn how to pray as an end in itself, or even to become a great orator of the things of God. Our goal is Him—not to know about Him, but to know Him.

As we deepen our intimacy with Christ, He makes us into disciples. Yes, it takes discipline on our part to become disciples. We are called to devote ourselves to prayer, study, and fellowship. But these tools are only the means through which the Lord draws us closer to Himself, for the essence of the whole process is to know His heart. He then lives His life through us and touches everyone who crosses our path. Simple, isn't it?

We will spend much time in the "Book" over the next several weeks. When God's Word is embraced for the purpose of knowing Christ's heart, and not for the purpose of intellectual stimulation, the results are incredible. We want to be people who not only talk a good game, but whose lifestyle is consistent with the commitment we have made to Christ in our hearts. I have met hoards of people who know the facts of the Bible but have no idea what it means to share intimacy with our Savior. Therefore, this course is not just a Bible study—not even a discipleship course. It is an endeavor that should change your whole life—every aspect of it, for He changes lives. The end result should be that you fall more deeply in love with Jesus Christ. (A tremendous difference lies between knowing Christ as Savior and falling in love with His heart.) As this relationship develops, the natural by-product is God's character lived out through your experience. Only then, does love, joy, peace, and everything else the world cannot have or attain become yours for the keeping. Also, as you grow, others are drawn to Him as you go about your normal routine, allowing Him to express His divine character through your unique personality. Then, you most definitely will have become His disciple.

God Himself—not the course—will make you into a disciple. However, we do trust that our time together will cause 2Timothy 2:2 to be fulfilled, to the greatest degree possible, in your experience.

Each week, during your time alone with God, you will answer questions relating to the

Scriptures or materials covered in that week's portion of the course. These questions are designed to be answered on a daily basis in an average of thirty to forty-five minutes per day. Also included are lessons that should supplement your answers to all the questions and tie everything that you have covered during the week together. Ideally these lessons should be read after you have answered the questions. However, if you still can't answer a particular question after exhausting all resources, feel free to read the portion of the lesson that pertains to that question.

We hope you find the course to be very practical and helpful in preparing you for discipleship. It doesn't contain as much theology as some of the other courses I have written (the Romans course). But it doesn't need the theology to accomplish its purpose.

New Testament reading assignments are placed at the end of each day's questions. You should read these assignments in the order specified in the course; their order will enhance your understanding of the questions and lesson covered each week. Be as diligent as possible in finishing what is assigned. You will not believe what a difference this perseverance will make... Trust me! You should record your new insights in a separate notebook.

In addition to your personal prayer and study, small groups will play a vital role in what we are trying to accomplish. (If your only alternative is to take the course by yourself, you will be fine. Just make sure that you hold yourself accountable to finish what you have started.) You should meet once each week in groups of six or less. (Note: If possible, try to form same-gender groups—men with men, and women with women. We have found that this arrangement works best. If this separation is not possible, mixing will be fine.) These small groups should retain the same people from week to week. You should meet in a home, church, or any other private location. Privacy is of utmost importance. Group meetings should normally last from 45 minutes to an hour, but allow flexibility—your group may want to meet for a shorter or longer time period. These groups give you an opportunity to pray together, share personal concerns, and discuss the questions and lesson covered in that week's material. Remember, we are coming together to minister to one another, as well as to learn from God's Word. No group should be so rigid that the Holy Spirit is prevented from doing His work.

One person in each group should be designated as the discussion leader. This responsibility should be rotated throughout the group from week to week so everyone will have an opportunity to fill this position. The discussion leader does not do the majority of the talking. His (or her) responsibility is to keep the group discussion on course.

You should begin your group meetings with prayer. After prayer, you can discuss the questions. The input from the group members should be the answers they have written down during the week. This keeps you on track and prevents the group from "chasing rabbits." If your group members aren't completing their assignments, your group will have little to discuss from the questions. Believe me, this format will hold everyone accountable. After you have finished discussing your answers, and if time permits, discuss the lesson, the weekly Scripture assignments, or anything else that the group decides is important.

Also, set a definite time to start your small group meetings and be on time. A disciple can learn discipline by fulfilling his commitment and being punctual. An outright emergency is the only excuse for missing your small-group meetings. Throughout the course we will be learning to put first things first, to persevere, and to be diligent; be faithful to your small groups with promptness and regular attendance.

Both *The Master Plan of Evangelism* (by Robert Coleman) and *Ordering Your Private World* (by Gordan MacDonald) will be covered in the latter part of the course. These books can be purchased at most Christian bookstores. I highly recommend these two resources.

You will also begin a prayer journal. This journal will contain both prayer requests and God's answers to them. It will be exciting to watch God honor your petitions. Your journal can be a notebook or any other resource that can be kept nearby.

Scripture memory will be a vital part of what we are trying to accomplish. We must begin to write God's Word on our heart (mind) if we desire to become disciples.

As we begin this journey, I pray that we might all arrive at a place of total surrender to the Lord Jesus. When this surrender occurs, we will become disciples. Remember Philippians 4:13!

Go to Week 1 and begin. Get ready to have fun!!

About Discipleship
(A, B, C, D, and E)

First Day—*Memorize Matthew 28:19* (Find the full list on page 175)

1. If you haven't done so already, read the course outline and introduction. Also, look through the maps located in the back of this booklet. Record your prayer requests in your prayer journal, each day this week.

2. What is your definition of a disciple?

Why do you think Jesus discipled only the twelve?

What impact do you think the time with Jesus had on the twelve?

3. Read John 1-2 and record your new insights in a separate notebook. Since you will be reading the entire New Testament during the next 19 weeks, try to designate a specific area in your notebook for each New Testament book. This process will allow you to use what you write down for future reference. I have recorded new insights in this manner for years, and have found it to be very profitable. We will read the Gospel of John first because it is a very basic book and one that will introduce you to how Jesus discipled the twelve. John, one of the twelve apostles, wrote: this Gospel; 1, 2, and 3John; and Revelation.

Second Day

1. What should a disciple of Christ desire above all else?

2. Do you think a large percentage of believers want to become disciples? If not, why not?

What hinders us most from becoming disciples?

3. Read John 3-4 and record new insights.

Third Day

1. Describe some personal concerns you have when you consider becoming a disciple.

2. From John 8:31, what does Jesus say about becoming a disciple?

What do you think He means by these statements?

3. From John 8:32, what does Jesus mean by "free"?

I thought disciple meant disciplined individual—not free individual. Is this true?

4. Read John 5 and record new insights.

Fourth Day—*Memorize Matthew 28:20* (Find the full list on page 175)

1. Why do you think it is important to sit with the Lord (in His Word and in prayer) on a regular basis?

List any Scripture that supports your answer?

2. List at least four men mentioned in God's Word who sat with the Lord on a regular basis.

How did the Lord choose to use them?

3. Read John 6 and record new insights.

Fifth Day

1. We can motivate ourselves in many ways to sit with the Lord—for instance, vow to study our Bibles on a daily basis—but what is the only motivation that will endure?

2. What would you tell a new Christian to help him begin to sit with the Lord?

Maybe you are a new Christian yourself. How will you start?

3. What does "abide" mean in John 15:7?

4. According to John 15:8, how do we "show ourselves" to be disciples?

5. Read John 7-8 and record new insights.

Sixth Day

1. If someone asked you how he should begin studying the Bible, with which book would you recommend he start?

If your answer was Leviticus, you automatically flunk the course—Ha! List the books you would have him read first—in order.

When you come to a verse that confuses you, what do you do?

2. Read this week's lesson, which starts on the next page, and record new insights below.

3. Read John 9-10 and record new insights.

About Discipleship
(A, B, C, D, and E)

A. The Importance of Discipleship

Many Christians want to become disciples but do not know how or where to start. The purpose of this course is to teach believers how to let Christ transform them into disciples, so He, through them, can make others into disciples.

Through discipleship the principle of multiplication, not addition, takes place in the Kingdom. Jesus is a perfect example: He poured His life into only twelve men, and as a result, the gospel spread throughout the world. After His resurrection, Jesus told them to make disciples of all nations (Matthew 28:19). And why did they obey? He had cultivated an intimate relationship with each one of them.

Yes, many people followed Jesus, and these multitudes were sometimes called disciples in the general sense; see Luke 6:17. But Jesus devoted most of His time to teaching just the twelve. He addressed and taught the multitudes, but He refused to work on the volume theory when it came to true discipleship. He knew that disciples are made in intense, personal, small-group situations.

You can never be a disciple if you do not desire to establish intimacy with "He who is your life" (Colossians 3:4). You must understand this principle from the outset. It takes time to become a disciple. It also takes testing, trials, and, yes, failure, but the end result is that you will experience the life that Jesus promised in John 10:10. In other words, He makes it worth our while. Becoming His disciple is merely knowing Him well enough to trust Him in all circumstances, so that He, in turn, might use you to transform other lives for His glory. Won't you let Him make you His disciple?

B. The Definition of a Disciple

Merriam Webster defines a disciple as "a pupil or follower of any teacher or school." Discipleship also means to be taught and to learn by practice or experience. So if we are to become disciples of Christ, we must become a pupil and follower of Christ.

C. The Life of Freedom Experienced by the Disciple

The word "disciple" scares most of us, but in essence discipleship leads to freedom—not imprisonment. The good news is Jesus Christ died to set us free, not to put us under bondage. The Christian life lived under bondage causes discouragement and defeat; the life of freedom in Christ brings power, authority, and rest. How, then, do we attain this freedom? Jesus said that the person who abides (stays, continues, dwells) in His Word will be His disciple (John 8:31). In the very next verse Jesus states what will happen in the disciple's life (v. 32). The disciple will know the truth, and the truth will set him free. Oh to be free! Free to let the Spirit of the living God direct our lives—no more slavery to the Law! This freedom is offered to every Christian but is only attained in the Christian experience by those who become true disciples.

D. The Importance of Learning to Sit with Christ

To "sit" with the Lord means to get alone with Him—Him and no one else—for the purpose of study, prayer, and fellowship. We must give the Lord time enough to teach us what He has done through Christ. Please do not try to make the Christian life fly by the power of your flesh (by your own strength). Rather, allow Him to reveal His very heart to you by spending time with Him. Sitting with the Lord also allows the Holy Spirit to build proper perspective into our lives. Only when you learn to view life from His perspective, which is the very definition of wisdom, will you indeed "live." In fact, only then will you find Him expressing His loving nature through your unique personality.

Jesus sat with the Father for thirty years preparing for three years of public ministry. Moses sat alone with God for forty years before he was ready to lead Israel out of Egypt. The apostle Paul sat in Arabia and Tarsus so he might walk in a manner worthy of His calling (Ephesians 4:1). King David, in Psalm 27:8, states that when the Lord told him to seek His face, he told the Lord: "Thy face, O Lord, I shall seek." God refers to David as a man after His own heart (1Samuel 13:14); because he sought the Lord's face (sat alone with Him), David knew Him in a very intimate way, and thus took on His character. Paul confirms that the same occurs in us when we sit with the Lord (read 2Corinthians 3:18).

Throughout Scripture, the great men of faith knew and understood the importance of getting alone with God. We will never become disciples until we are grounded in this truth ourselves. The only motivation that will last is sheer love for Christ. If our motivation to sit with Him is based on anything else, it will soon vanish away.

E. Learning To Sit with Christ

You may ask, "But how do I learn to sit with Him?" One of the main things to understand is that an appetite for God's Word is developed by starting with realistic goals. We wouldn't prepare to run a race by running ten miles the first day of training. If we did, we would have no motivation to run the next day—that is if we were still alive! It is the same with learning to sit with Christ. We must start with realistic goals and build. One of the main objectives of this course is that you learn how to set such goals and begin to attain them.

In John 15:7-8, Jesus states that His disciples will bear fruit. Fruit is a natural byproduct of discipleship, but no disciple bears fruit unless he is abiding in Jesus and His Word. "Abiding" means to be in close or settled union. To abide in Christ is to be in close fellowship with Him, trusting Him to fulfill the truth of His Word in our lives. As we learn to sit with Him, the Holy Spirit, through the written Word, teaches us how to abide. For the Christian, sitting is equivalent to filling your car with gas. No gas, no power! As we know Him more intimately we begin to bear fruit, thus proving to be His disciples.

Most of us know little about the Bible when we first come to Christ. Therefore, we start reading the Bible the way we read any book. We begin with Genesis and go straight through. We do fine for a few days, but when we reach Leviticus we usually give up and quit. Leviticus in the Old Testament is like Revelation in the New Testament. It should be read after much time has been spent in the more basic books.

A new student of the Bible should start in the four Gospels: Matthew, Mark, Luke, and John. He could then study Philippians, Galatians, 1 & 2Corinthians, 1John, and some of the more basic epistles. Romans is a good book on which to concentrate, especially the first eight chapters. When you understand Romans 1-8, the Bible genuinely comes alive. Your study in the New Testament should end, not begin, with Revelation.

Genesis is a good Old Testament book with which to begin, along with Exodus. Joshua and Judges would be good to read next, followed by 1 & 2Samuel and 1 & 2Kings (don't let all the names of the kings scare you.) Psalms and Proverbs are excellent to read on a daily basis—maybe a chapter out of each per day.

Regardless of what portion of the Bible we study, we must continually remember this principle: If we read something that is difficult to understand, we should just keep reading. The understanding will come later as we mature in the faith. The Bible explains itself if we give it the time and the opportunity. A God of all wisdom wrote it, and knowing the God of all wisdom is necessary to understand it (Philippians 3:10).

We never sit with the Lord for the purpose of intellectual stimulation. Even Satan knows and can quote Scripture (Matthew 4:6). Furthermore, many people who can talk the Christian language haven't the slightest idea how to live out the Christian walk. Our goal in sitting is to know His heart.

Another advantage in sitting is that as the disciple prayerfully reads the Word of God, his prayer is enhanced beyond comprehension (Ephesians 6:10-18). And when we learn to be effective prayer warriors—WATCH OUT!

We are by no means saying that we place ourselves under Law in studying God's Word. We are free in Christ, and we must constantly keep this knowledge in the forefront of our minds. We must never study God's Word out of obligation, but rather, simply because we love Him. I have never seen two people in love who did not do everything they could to be alone with each other. See my point?

You have now completed week one. Ask the Lord to give you a desire to use what you have learned to encourage others.

The Life of Moses
(A and B)

First Day—*Memorize Matthew 6:24* (Find the full list on page 175)

1. Read Exodus chapters 2-4, and write down any new insights below.

2. Who named Moses?

What does his name mean? (Hint: The definition of his name is in Exodus 2:10.)

3. After Moses grew up physically, did he do anything to indicate that he had not forgotten his Hebrew heritage?

If so, what did he do?

Did Moses, at this time, realize that God would use him to deliver his people (Acts 7:23-25)?

4. How did his Hebrew brethren respond to Moses's actions?

Why do you think they responded in this manner?

How did Pharaoh respond?

5. Read John 11-12 and record new insights in your notebook. Write down any new prayer requests in your prayer journal, each day this week. Also list all answered prayer.

Second Day

1. Read Exodus 2. Had you been Moses, what would you have been thinking as you departed from Egypt? Be very honest and open in answering this question.

2. Read Hebrews 11:23-27 to discover Moses's perspective as he left Egypt. Meditate a few minutes on Hebrews 11:25-27. What did you learn from these passages that can help you when dealing with unpleasant circumstances?

3. Where did Moses settle after he left Egypt?

Find this location on the map titled, *From Egypt to Canaan,* in the back of the course.

4. From Exodus 2:15, what was the first thing that Moses did when he arrived in Midian? (Hint: Notice a familiar word in the last phrase of this verse.)

Do you think God had anything to do with Moses being placed in these "unpleasant" circumstances?
Explain.

What do God's actions say to you about the importance that God places on being alone with Him?

5. What was Moses's occupation in Midian?

Did he own his own business?

Why would God allow Moses to have such a "low-class" job?

6. What does Exodus 2:23-25 teach you about prayer?

According to verse 24, what did God remember that caused Him to notice Israel (v. 25)?

Is a believer in covenant with God (Matthew 26:26-28 and Luke 22:20)?

Why should this covenant encourage us in our prayer life (Hebrews 4:16)?

How can a non-believer enter into this covenant?

7. Read John 13-14 and record new insights.

Third Day

1. Read Exodus 3. According to verse 1, where was Moses pasturing Jethro's flock?

What happened in verses 2-3 that caught Moses's attention?

How did God describe Himself as He addressed Moses in verse 6?

Why would He describe Himself in this manner?

2. From verses 7-10, what did God desire to do with Moses?

How did Moses respond to God's request (v. 11)?

What do you see different about the Moses described here and the Moses in Exodus 2:11-12?

What brought on the change?

3. What promises did God make to Moses in verse 12?

How would you have responded had God made these promises to you?

A continued study of the life of Moses will reveal that God fulfilled these promises in a very supernatural way to the greatest degree possible.

4. Do you always feel adequate to carry out God's calling on your life?

If not, how can this inadequacy work in your favor (tie in this answer with James 4:6)?

5. Read John 15-16. Record your new insights in your notebook.

Fourth Day—*Memorize Matthew 6:33* (Find the full list on page 175)
1. Read Exodus 4:1-31. Do you really think that God failed to realize what Moses was holding in his hand (Exodus 4:2)?

Why would God focus on Moses's staff?

2. What did God ask Moses to do with his staff (Exodus 4:3)?

What does this request symbolize?

How does this idea apply to your own walk with the Lord?

3. What happened to Moses's hand when he placed it in his bosom and removed it (v. 6)?

What happened when he placed it in his bosom a second time and removed it (v. 7)? (This hand was the one that would hold God's staff.)

What does this event communicate to you about the importance of having hands that are submitted to the Lord?

4. Read John 17-18 and write down any new insights.

Fifth Day

1. Read Exodus 4:1-31. What happened to Moses's staff when he threw it to the ground?

How did he respond (v. 3)?

What is the spiritual significance of his response?

2. When was the serpent turned back into a staff (v. 4)?

How would you have responded had God asked you to pick up the serpent?

Whose staff was it after Moses picked it up (Exodus 4:20)?

What does this ownership say to you about the importance of giving all things to God?

3. Read John 19-20 and record new insights.

Sixth Day

1. List a few things that God did with His staff, now that it belonged to Him.

Would you like to possess such a staff?

If so, what would you do with it?

2. As God prepared Moses to lead the Israelites, do you think Moses ever imagined what the future held for him?

Explain your answer.

Can God open doors of service for you after you have matured in the faith?

After studying this portion of Moses's life, what will need to occur in your life before He can use you effectively?

3. Read this week's lesson and record any new insights.

4. Read John 21 and record new insights in your notebook.

The Life of Moses
(A and B)

A. Moses' Early Life (First Forty Years)

We start reading about the life of Moses in Exodus 2. Because his parents were children of Levi, Moses was a Hebrew from an important tribe (v. 1). When he was born Pharaoh had ordered all Hebrew sons to be killed at birth (Exodus 1:22). So Moses's mother hid him for three months, then placed him in a basket among the reeds by the bank of the Nile (Exodus 2:2-3). As his sister stood watch, Pharaoh's daughter came to bathe at the Nile and saw the baby among the reeds. Although she realized he was a Hebrew, she had pity on him. Moses's sister asked Pharaoh's daughter if she could call a nurse from the Hebrew women. Pharaoh's daughter agreed, so Moses's sister called her and Moses's own mother to nurse him (Exodus 2:4-9). What an illustration of God's sovereignty!

When the baby grew, he was brought to Pharaoh's daughter. She named him Moses, which means "to draw out," because she had drawn him out of the water of the Nile (v. 10).

From a worldly or human viewpoint, Moses might have been delighted to live in this situation for the rest of his life. After all, he could have any material possession or pleasure he desired. He could say "jump" to his servants, and their only reply would be "how high?" He "had it made." But Moses was a Hebrew, and once a Hebrew, always a Hebrew.

Moses grew up (physical growth, not spiritual), and went out to visit his people, who at the time were slaves of the Egyptians. When one of the Egyptians began beating a fellow Hebrew, Moses killed the Egyptian and hid his body in the sand (Exodus 2:11-12). Acts 7:23-25 relates that Moses realized his calling. He was to deliver his people, but he first had to learn some very important lessons about leadership and how God desired His work to be accomplished.

This story provides us with some essential information relating to discipleship. Moses thought he was serving God by striking down the Egyptian. The Egyptian was taking advantage of one of God's chosen people. I am convinced that Moses went home delighted over what he had done "for God." But the Scriptures indicate that God was not happy with Moses's response. I envision the Lord saying, "Now look at Moses. I really love him, but bless his heart, he is trying to serve Me in his own strength. He is trying to do things for Me, when all I require of him is that he let Me do My work through him. I see a need to get him alone with Me. I think I will have Moses move to Midian, and I think I will use Pharaoh to convince him that he needs to move" (Exodus 2:13-15). (To comprehend Moses's attitude as God led him away from Egypt, read Hebrews 11:24-27. Moses had a heart for God.)

God saw much potential in Moses, but Moses needed to know his God more intimately. The first thing Moses did in Midian was sit (read the last phrase of Exodus 2:15). He stopped doing and started sitting. What circumstance is God allowing to cross your path to cause you to slow down? The opportunity for ministry will come, but we must first know our God and be equipped with His Word. It takes humility to let God do His work through you, rather than you doing it for Him. In our next section God builds humility into Moses's life through his experiences in Midian.

B. How Moses Became a Disciple (Second 40 Years)

Moses took a wife while in Midian (Exodus 2:16-22). Matrimony will build humility into any man. No, seriously, I am not sure what kind of marriage Moses and Zipporah had, for Scripture says very little about it. One passage suggests that their relationship was somewhat stormy (Exodus 4:25). God can use such situations to teach any man (or woman) a vast amount of truth.

Moses was also a shepherd (Exodus 3:1). The flock belonged to his father-in-law—a fact that must have further humbled Moses. But after Moses had been alone with his Lord for forty years, God appeared to him in a bush at the base of Horeb, or Mount Sinai (v. 1). Moses was intrigued that the bush was on fire but was not consumed (v. 2). God's presence was in the bush, for when God shows up, glory, in the form of fire or a cloud, is usually manifested (because God is so holy and pure).

God introduced Himself as the God of Abraham, Isaac, and Jacob (v. 6) so Moses would trust every word that He stated. God then told Moses that he was to lead His people out of Egypt (vv. 7-10). But can you believe Moses's response in verse 11? He felt totally inadequate to do so, the very response for which God had been waiting. Moses' response confirmed that he no longer trusted in himself, as he had done earlier in Exodus 2:11-12, and was a vessel through which God's power could flow to accomplish His work. Simply stated, Moses was finally a broken man. God then promised to go with him and bring him back to Mount Sinai after His people had been delivered (v. 12). God fulfilling these promises in the next several chapters will be exciting to watch. What transpires should cause anyone to seek to be a broken vessel.

God had allowed almost everything to be taken from Moses that might distract him from focusing solely on Him. (This example does not mean that a man cannot own material possessions and be God's disciple; these possessions need to be viewed from God's perspective.) However, Moses still owned a staff; how the Lord took this staff is a wonderful object lesson for any of us who want to follow Christ. Many things could be stated about this segment of Moses's life, but for the sake of time and space we will focus solely on the staff.

The staff was one of Moses's few possessions that had not yet been given to the Lord. In Exodus 4:2, God asks Moses, "What is that in your hand?" Moses answers, "A staff." Because God wanted Moses to understand what his staff symbolized as long as it belonged to Moses, He asked him to throw it to the ground (Exodus 4:3). God changed Moses's staff into a serpent because He wanted Moses to see what his staff represented as long as it remained the source of Moses's security.

In Moses's day every shepherd owned a staff, one purpose of which was to fight off the flock's enemies. The staff also was a tool to help control the flock. However, it was Moses's enemy if it kept him from trusting God to meet his needs.

Moses fled when the staff became a serpent. Has God ever taken something very dear to you—that was not dear to Him—and allowed you to view it from His perspective? Didn't it scare you later to realize that you wanted it in the first place? Is there something that God has asked you to throw down: maybe a sinful habit, a relationship, an emotional wound, or an unhealthy attitude? If you will but turn it loose, He will prove that it was not His best for your life. If you have never tried letting go, I challenge you to do so now. The Lord's grace will sustain you until He shows you the reason you were to lay it down.

After He had turned Moses's staff into a serpent, God told him to pick it up, not by the head, but by the tail. Now if we had been Moses, we might have thought, "The head is the biting end Lord, and if I pick the serpent up by the tail it will bite me for sure. If I have to pick it up, can't I at least choose which end to go for?"

Moses, however, had learned to trust God during his forty years at Midian. He picked up the serpent by the tail; Scripture says that when Moses caught it, the serpent became a staff in his hand (Exodus 4:4). But the staff was now God's staff, for in Exodus 4:20 it is referred to for the first time as "the staff of God." And what role would the staff now play under its new Owner? Read the following verses for the answer: Exodus 4:17, 7:9-12, 7:14-21, 8:5-6, 8:16-17, 9:23, 10:13, 14:16,17:5-6, and 17:8-13. We will discuss these verses in our next section.

God had Moses place his hand into his bosom (Exodus 4:6). When he took it out it was leprous like snow (v. 6). This action too could point to what Moses's hand (the hand that would hold the staff) represented as long as it was not under the authority of the Lord. After placing this same hand back into his bosom, it came out restored (v. 7). Thus Moses's hand was now the Lord's hand, to hold the Lord's staff. Everything was in order. The mission could now be accomplished.

Have you given God your talent, your abilities, your desires, your dreams, your fears, your weaknesses, that He might use them for His glory? Moses's staff would have remained an ordinary staff had Moses not given it to the Lord. In the same way, his hand would have remained an ordinary hand had it not been submitted to the Lord. Therefore, our abilities will remain ordinary abilities until we surrender them to Jesus Christ.

Let's now reflect back to Exodus 2:23-25. The king of Egypt had just died, and the sons of Israel (the Hebrews) were crying to God because of their bondage. God heard them and remembered the promises He had made to Abraham, Isaac, and Jacob. God had promised Abraham, the father of the Hebrews, that his offspring would become a great nation (Genesis 12:1-3) that would inherit the "Promised Land" (Genesis 13:14-17). God had carried down these promises through Isaac (Genesis 26:2-5) and Jacob (Genesis 35:10-12). Had the Lord been preparing someone to lead His nation out of Egypt? Of course He had, and the amazing thing is that He had been doing it for forty years. He had groomed Moses all of this time for this very moment. This instance illustrates the degree to which God has everything under control. Moses's original vision of leading God's people had died (remember Acts 7:23-25). God would now resurrect this vision and fulfill it to the greatest degree possible. Has God allowed your vision to die? Does this death mean that He can't resurrect it? Of course not!

You may be thinking: "There is no way that God can use me. I have no extraordinary abilities or talents." The good news is that God knows where He can use you, but, like Moses, He first requires that you establish intimacy with Him. He then opens doors of service that are beyond anything you could imagine. While Moses was in Midian, do you think he had aspirations of leading Israel? Never! But God, because He knows everything in the past and the future, knew he would lead Israel, even before Moses was born. Isn't that exciting?

We will watch the Lord place Moses into service in next week's lesson. Moses's sitting in Midian paid huge dividends as he led Israel out of Egypt. It should be a fun week, so come back ready to learn. You are growing!

The Life of Moses
(C, 1)

First Day—*Memorize 1Timothy 6:7* (Find the full list on page 175)

1. Read Exodus 5:1-23. How did Pharaoh react to Moses's suggestion?

How did the Hebrew people then react to Moses?

How do you think Moses felt after this series of events?

How would you have felt?

2. Read Exodus 14. Where did Israel want to go when they saw Pharaoh pursuing them (vv. 10-12)?

How does this account relate to the Christian experience?

Have you ever wanted to go back to Egypt (back to where you were before you met Christ)?

What held you back?

3. We will now start reading the book of Acts and finish it by the time we begin our study of the life of Paul (in week 5). Examining Acts will equip you to dig deeper into Paul's life once we get there. Take advantage of the maps located in the back of the course, especially when you study Paul's missionary journeys and his trip to Rome. Luke wrote the book of Acts as well as the Gospel of Luke. He was a traveling companion of Paul and a Gentile. He was with Paul during his first (Colossians 4:14, Philemon 24) and second (2Timothy 4:11) imprisonments in Rome. He was not one of the original twelve apostles. Read Acts 1-2 and write down your new insights. Write down any new prayer requests in your prayer journal, each day this week. Also list all answered prayer.

Second Day

1. Read Exodus 14. God sent several judgments upon Egypt between Exodus 5 and Exodus 14. These judgments finally caused Pharaoh to allow Israel passage from Egypt. Through what means did God deliver Israel from Pharaoh once Israel departed (Exodus 14)?

What was Israel's reaction after the Lord delivered them (Exodus 14:31)?

2. Read Exodus 15. What was Israel's next problem?

How did the people react to Moses?

What was Moses's reaction?

Does this incident point to Christ in any way?

3. Read Acts 3-4, and record new insights in your notebook.

Third Day

1. Read Exodus 16. What was Israel's problem now?

Who got the blame?

Where did the people still desire to go (v. 3)?

What was the Lord's solution?

How does His solution point to Jesus (John 6:30-35)?

2. Read Exodus 17:1-7. What was Israel's problem?

Who got the blame?

What was God's solution?

How does this solution point to Jesus (1Corinthians 10:4, John 4:13-14, 7:37-39)?

3. Read Acts 5-6 and record new insights.

Fourth Day—*Memorize 1Timothy 6:8* (Find the full list on page 175)

1. Read Numbers 13 and 14. Israel had moved from Mt Sinai to a location south of the border of the land of Canaan (to Kadesh-Barnea-Numbers 32:8-9).

Find Kadesh Barnea on the map titled ***From Egypt to Canaan.*** How did the people respond to the reports given by the twelve spies?

From what is stated in Numbers 14:2, would you say that man normally desires to stay where he is spiritually (desires to die in the wilderness), or that he desires to go on to maturity (and face the challenges in Canaan)?

Why is this desire the case?

Which have you chosen to do, and why?

2. What impressed you about Joshua and Caleb?

How did God respond when Israel wanted to stone Moses (Numbers 14:11-12)?

How did Moses then respond (Numbers 14:13-19)?

Would you have handled God's proposition the way Moses did?
Explain.

3. Read Acts 7-8 and record new insights.

Fifth Day

1. Read Numbers 20. What was the problem?

Where did the people still desire to go (vv. 1-5)?

2. How did Moses disobey (vv. 6-13)?

What do you learn from the fact that Moses disobeyed after so many years of obedience?

What would be the consequences of his disobedience?

What does this account teach you about the crucifixion of Jesus?

3. Was Moses bitter over not being allowed to enter Canaan with his people? (Use Scripture to support your answer.)

Do you think he completely understood his punishment? Explain.

Challenge Question: Was he ever allowed to enter the land?

4. Read Acts 9-10 and record new insights.

Sixth Day

1. Read Numbers 13:30. Can we approach the circumstances we face with this type of attitude?

If so, explain how it can be done.

2. Read this week's lesson. Record any new insights below.

3. Read Acts 11-12 and record new insights in your notebook

The Life of Moses
(C, 1)

C. Moses' Life as a Disciple (Last 40 Years)

1. How Moses Led Israel

Most of us are familiar with this portion of Moses's life. I will never forget the first time I studied this section of Scripture. I was a new Christian eager to serve and glorify the Lord, but I knew nothing about walking with Him. All I knew was that Moses had a powerful staff and that I wanted one just like it. I had enough insight to know they weren't sold at J.C. Penney, but I felt if I looked hard and long enough I would eventually find one. I so desperately wanted God to use me the same way He had used Moses.

In my immaturity I had failed to consider one major point: the breaking process that Moses experienced before he could be trusted with God's staff. As Christians, we often want God to use us, but our flesh does not want to be broken. The flesh wants to lead, by telling people how to run their lives, rather than taking the road that leads to humility (Numbers 12:3). The flesh wants to do "for God" so it can receive glory, but it forgets that God is a jealous God who wants—and is worthy to receive—all the glory for Himself (Exodus 34:14). We have seen how the Lord broke Moses. So let's examine what He can do with a man of humility.

Many think they would have enjoyed walking in Moses's shoes (sandals). Just think of the notoriety and power that came with his position of authority. But Moses had no idea what it meant to suffer until he was sent from Midian to Egypt

First, he was ridiculed, not only by Pharaoh, but also by his own people (Exodus 5:1-23). Now read Exodus 14:1-19. The Hebrews had just been released to offer sacrifices, but when they departed, Pharaoh pursued them to the Red Sea. The people blamed Moses for their problems (vv. 10-13). But the man leading the nation had sat one-on-one with the Lord for forty years. As a result, Moses could view life from God's perspective. I love Moses's response in verses 13 and 14. He knew the Lord would destroy the enemy and fight for the Hebrew nation even while they kept silent. Without his training in Midian, he probably would have called a board meeting to figure out a plan, a plan that would have meant certain disaster. But now he knew intimately the God who had promised deliverance, which caused him to place zero trust in the strength of man or man's wisdom.

Every disciple must learn this lesson. We can never deliver anyone, not even ourselves. Only God is capable of bringing deliverance. Exodus 14:15-31 provides further evidence that God honored Moses's faith. This incident greatly affected the people under Moses's authority (v. 31). They finally believed in the Lord and in His servant Moses.

Any disciple who is placed in a leadership role will be tested, not only by enemies, but also by friends. Consequently, a new Christian should never be given a leadership role in the church (1Timothy 3:6). Only after he has been tried and has had an opportunity to mature will people welcome his instruction. God used His staff to deliver His people at the Red Sea. New Christians possess a staff, but in most cases it still belongs to them personally. Moses's life has taught us that the staff that belongs to us is of little use to the Lord. However, as we seek to know our God in an intimate kind of way, our staff becomes His staff!

Moses' popularity prevailed until Israel faced another problem (Exodus 15:22-24). This time they were without good water. They grumbled against Moses (v. 24) and Moses did what every disciple should do when faced with a problem: He prayed (v. 25). Oh, how the disciple must learn to seek God in the midst of every hardship. A tree was used to make the water sweet. The tree (cross) of Christ truly makes life sweet to those who accept (by faith) what occurred there.

Again in Exodus 16:1-3 the Israelites grumbled. This time they were hungry and without food. And guess who got the blame? You guessed it: Moses! Moses told the people that their grumblings were not against Aaron or him, but against the Lord (v. 8). Are you starting to see the price that must be paid by those placed in leadership positions?

Moses had learned to give his burdens to the Lord, which allowed him to view his circumstances from God's perspective. Had he not learned this lesson in Midian, he would have wilted mentally or emotionally in the heat of the battle. A disciple must learn to give every burden to Christ (1Peter 5:7). As a result of Moses' trust, the Lord sent manna and quail from heaven (Exodus 16:4-34); this manna, which pointed to Christ (John 6:30-35), fed them for their forty years in the wilderness (v. 35).

Soon after, the Israelites faced another water shortage (Exodus 17:1), so naturally they grumbled against Moses (vv. 2-3). Had I been Moses I probably would have been thinking, "Hey God, I know you promised to take us to the land of milk and honey (Exodus 3:6-8), but why all this turmoil along the way?" But Moses, unlike many, sought the advice of the Lord (Exodus 17:4), and the remedy was revealed (vv. 5-6). His forty years of getting to know and trust God paid off, for the Lord's staff—the one that formerly belonged to Moses—brought forth the waters of deliverance.

This section of Scripture is fascinating, for it draws a picture of the crucifixion of Christ. 1Corinthians 10:4 tells that the rock was Christ. Moses was to strike the rock with the staff of God (Exodus 17:5-6) and water was to spring forth for the people. Jesus said He would give living water to anyone who would receive it (John 4:10-14, 7:37-39). Therefore, when Moses (a Jew) struck the rock (Christ), his action symbolized what the Jewish (Hebrew) nation would do to Jesus. They would have Him crucified, but as a result, living water (God's Spirit) would spring forth to all who would receive it. Clearly, the Old Testament is filled with Jesus! As we mature in the faith and in His Word, the Lord will show us more of Christ in every book of the Bible. No matter what section of Scripture we read, we must always look for Jesus.

God's people moved north toward the land of Canaan (follow this journey on the map titled *From Egypt to Canaan*). Israel was camping in Kadesh, located just outside the southern border of Canaan, and the people had received the not-so-rosy report from the twelve spies (Numbers 13). When they heard the report, they grumbled against Moses and desired to return to Egypt or else die in the wilderness (Numbers 14:2). (If we are not careful, we will desire to stay at the maturity level that we have attained and not pay the price that it takes to enter the land—to go on to maturity. We, many times, either want to go back to Egypt or die where we are.) Read Moses and Aaron's response in Numbers 14:5 and Joshua and Caleb's response in Numbers 14:6-9. (Also refer back to Caleb's response in Numbers 13:30.) These responses were based totally on faith; they had nothing to do with the circumstance of the hour. As disciples, we can respond to adversity in this manner if we will but yield to God's promises. However, the Israelites still desired to stone them (Numbers 14:10).

No section of Scripture reveals more of Moses' heart than Numbers 14:11-19. You might think that Moses would have been delighted with God's idea of replacing Israel with a greater and mightier nation. But Moses had spent forty years at the feet of his God. His response, therefore, was based on his unconditional love for the Lord and His people. Because Moses so loved the Lord, he was naturally concerned about His reputation, as well as His people. Consequently, he asked the Lord to pardon Israel (vv. 13-19). The Lord's response to Moses' request is given in verse 20; "I have pardoned them according to your word."

A disciple must love God's people with unconditional love, or else the temptation to "trade them in" will be too much to bear. (God would never have destroyed Israel, regardless of Moses' response. He had made several unconditional promises to the nation that He was obligated to fulfill.) I cannot help but believe that God's suggestion in Numbers 14:11-12 was solely for Moses' benefit.

Up to now, Moses has responded to crisis after crisis with unwavering faith. Thus, it is hard to believe that a man of Moses' caliber could commit blatant sin. But any disciple is capable of faltering in times of weakness. To confirm that Moses was very much flesh and blood, the Lord has given us Numbers 20:1-12. The people were still in Kadesh, still without water, still blaming Moses and Aaron for their problems, and still desiring to return to Egypt. Moses and Aaron, however, continued to seek the Lord's guidance (v. 6). God instructed Moses to take the Lord's staff and speak to the rock in front of the congregation of Israel (vv. 7-8). Sounds pretty simple, doesn't it?

Let's stop for a moment and consider Moses' dilemma. He had given his life to these people, and they refused to obey. In fact, his efforts seemed totally in vain. This predicament can be devastating to a leader, and in many cases can become an Achilles heel. At these times he must be aware of the enemy's tactics and refuse the enemy's lie. If not, his situation will look hopeless, and failure is inevitable. Most likely Moses felt this distress, so instead of responding, he reacted. Instead of speaking to the rock, he struck the rock, and water came forth abundantly.

Now to many, Moses' sin would have been of such minor proportions that it would have gone unnoticed. After all, what is the difference in striking a rock and speaking to a rock? Moses hadn't killed someone or robbed a bank. And besides, water came forth, and the people drank their fill—no harm done. What was all the fuss about? But in God's economy it was a big deal. An act of disobedience had occurred, an act with which He had to deal.

According to Psalm 106:33, Moses spoke rashly with his lips, which means that instead of responding to the situation, he reacted. As a result, he called the people rebels (Numbers 20:10), and said, "shall we bring forth water for you out of this rock?" He said, "shall we bring forth water?" This statement reveals Moses's problem, for instead of allowing God to bring forth the water, Moses took the task upon himself. Also, according to verse 12, Moses was guilty of unbelief and guilty of not treating God as holy in the sight of Israel. Therefore, a sin of great magnitude had been committed.

The penalty is given in verse 12. Moses was restricted from entering Canaan; many people view this penalty as too severe considering Moses' track record. But Scripture indicates that He agreed with God's decision and went on about his business. He did, on one occasion, seek permission to enter the land (Deuteronomy 3:23-25). However, when the Lord refused (v. 26), he accepted God's response with no questions. Moses was allowed to enter the land in Matthew 17:1-3—when Jesus was transfigured. I am certain that had He been given the choice of entering the land with his people, or entering it later when the Messiah was on earth, he would have chosen the latter. Isn't our God faithful!

Nothing mentioned indicates that Moses was angry or upset with God. Even in Numbers 27:12-14, when God revealed to Moses that he was to die, his only concern was that a capable leader be appointed to oversee Israel (Numbers 27:15-17).

(Also read Deuteronomy 32:4, in fact read all of Deuteronomy 32 if time permits. Moses wrote this song shortly before his death.) Moses did not request that his life be prolonged (Deuteronomy 34:1-5). His silence speaks volumes about his character. Moses knew and trusted God's heart. His trust didn't mean that he understood all the details of his penalty, but deep inside he knew that God had everything under control.

Has God allowed you to walk in a circumstance that you did not understand? Did you find yourself grumbling at God or resting in Him as you walked through it? Since Romans 8:28 is true, one of the great lessons a disciple must learn is the lesson of trust.

Our Lord truly is in charge, no matter how we perceive the situations of life. To put the finishing touches on this section, we will take a minute to examine what Moses' act of disobedience symbolized. In Exodus 17:6, Moses was asked to strike the rock. We have already confirmed that this act symbolized the crucifixion of Christ. But in Numbers 20:8, God asked Moses to speak to the rock, not strike the rock. Instead, he struck the rock twice (Numbers 20:11). God's judgment on Moses confirms that Jesus could only be crucified once (1Peter 3:18). He died once for all sin (Hebrews 10:12), and nothing could cause Him to be crucified again. Are you starting to see that Jesus is contained in the Old Testament, but is explained in the New? The Book is a story of Jesus from cover to cover.

Next week you will learn how Moses discipled Joshua. Come back ready to go!

The Life of Moses
(C, 2)

First Day

1. Read Exodus 17:8-16. What was Israel's problem?

Who did Moses select to take care of the problem? Moses disciples this man throughout the remainder of his life.

What did Moses do while on the hill?

What do his actions teach you about the importance of praying for those you are discipling?

2. What does the account of Exodus 17:8-16 teach you about the importance of intercessory prayer? This significance is why we appreciate your prayers so much. Thanks.

3. Read Exodus 24:12-14. When Moses went up to hear from God, who went with him?

What does this accompaniment tell you about the depth of Moses and Joshua's relationship?

4. Read Exodus 32:15-18. Who was with Moses when he came off Mount Sinai with the Ten Commandments?

What did Joshua say about the noise he heard from the camp (v. 17)?

What did Moses then say about the noise from the camp (v. 18)?

Can we help others to properly interpret what they are hearing?

How does Hebrews 5:11-14 relate to this question?

5. What is the main thing you have learned from today's questions?

Are you starting to see that discipleship is basically spending time with those whom you view as faithful and allowing them to observe your walk with Christ? Discipleship isn't so difficult!

6. Read Acts 13-14 and record new insights in your notebook. Use the map titled *Paul's First Missionary Journey*.

Second Day

1. Read Exodus 33:7-11. What was the purpose of the tent of meeting?

What happened each time Moses entered the tent of meeting?

What did the people do?

2. What is said about Joshua in Exodus 33:11?

Joshua had learned the importance of sitting alone with his God. Guess who taught him? Of all the things that Moses taught Joshua, this lesson was the most significant. Why was this behavior such a crucial thing for Joshua to learn?

From our earlier lessons, what had occurred in Moses' life that had shown him his need for more sitting and less doing?

How has your time alone with God impacted your life recently?

3. Read Acts 15-16 and record new insights.

Third Day—*Memorize Matthew 10:39*
1. Read Numbers 13:1-16, 25-33, and 14:1-10. Would you say that Joshua's involvement with Moses had caused Joshua to be radically different from the rest of his brethren (aside from Caleb)?

What does this difference tell you about the importance of discipleship?

2. Read Numbers 27:12-23. In your opinion, why would God choose Joshua to succeed Moses?

Had you been Moses, would you have been pleased with God's choice?
Why?

Do these events encourage you to become a disciple and to convey what you have learned to others?
Explain.

3. Read Acts 17-18 and record new insights.

Fourth Day

1. Skim over Deuteronomy chapters 1, 3, 31 and 34. Once again observe Moses' impact on Joshua's life, especially in Deuteronomy 34:9. How does this effect tie in with what we are trying to accomplish in this course?

2. Read Acts 19-20 and record new insights. Are you using the maps supplied with the course?

Fifth Day

1. Read Joshua 1:1. Who spoke to Joshua?

What had taken place in Joshua's life that had prepared him to hear? (Do not make this question harder than it actually is.)

2. Read Joshua 1:1-18 and be encouraged as you observe the fruit of discipleship in Joshua's life. Write down some of your thoughts.

What does Joshua 1:8 communicate about the importance of God's Word in the disciple's life?

You should read the entire book of Joshua at some point in the not-too-distant future.

3. Read Judges 2:6-8. What do these verses say about Joshua's ability to disciple others?

Now read Judges 2:10. Did the disciples of Joshua disciple anyone?

What resulted?

What does this situation communicate to you?

4. Read Judges 2:11 and answer the following questions. What is the natural byproduct of a society that refuses to learn truth?

Does this knowledge stimulate you to reach out and disciple those around you?

If so, why? If not, why not?

5. Read Acts 21-22 and record new insights.

Sixth Day

1. Read this week's lesson and write down any new insights.

2. Read Acts 23-25 and record new insights in your notebook.

The Life of Moses
(C, 2)

C. Moses' Life as a Disciple (Last Forty Years)

  2. How Moses Discipled Joshua

Few places in Scripture communicate more about discipleship than Exodus 17-Deuteronomy 34. Here we learn of Moses and Joshua, and how their time together molded Joshua into a man of God. This lesson illustrates that discipleship is vital but can be done in a very natural way, without programs and rigid guidelines.

Joshua is first mentioned in Exodus 17:9. In Exodus 17:8-14 Israel is confronted with another problem. Amalek, an enemy, came against Israel at Rephidim. But once again God will use Moses and His staff to deliver His people. Moses told Joshua (the man who would guide Israel after Moses' death—the man who Moses was discipling) to choose men to fight against Amalek. Moses would station himself on a hill with the staff of God (v. 9).

Many may have wondered why Moses chose to stay on the hill rather than to fight alongside Joshua. After all, if he was going to be a "real" man, he should at least have the courage to enter the battle. However, the true battle took place on the hill, not in the valley. Moses' responsibility was to raise the staff of God. As long as it was raised, the momentum of the battle was with Israel (v. 11). When his hand grew weary, the momentum swung to Amalek (v. 11).

This scene is a vivid picture of the power of intercessory prayer. Moses believed that the Lord would deliver Israel; thus, he stayed on the hill seeking God's blessing. And sure enough, as he interceded, the battle was won. All Joshua did in the valley was capture the spoil that Moses had won on the hill. But Moses grew weary from holding the staff (vv. 11-12). Only after Aaron and Hur assisted him did Israel prevail.

We must pray for those we are called to disciple. They must also be given opportunities to lead men against the enemy. Jesus sent the 70 out two-by-two (Luke 10:1-16). When they returned, they said, "Lord, even the demons are subject to us in Your name" (Luke 10:17). Jesus then said, "I was watching Satan fall from heaven like lightning" (Luke 10:18). Jesus had given them authority over the powers of darkness (Luke 10:19). But they had to face the enemy head-on before they could realize what they possessed in Jesus. Moses prayed God's blessings upon Joshua, and Joshua prevailed. As we pray, those we are pouring our lives into will prevail as well.

Men were present to support Moses in time of need; Aaron and Hur assisted him as he prayed from the hill (Exodus 17:12). This same thing happened with Paul. Paul constantly prayed for those he had instructed (Ephesians 1:15-19; Philippians 1:3-4), and faithful men and women were by his side whenever he needed them (2Timothy 4:11, Romans 16:3-4). God will do the same for us.

Joshua is mentioned next in Exodus 24:12-14. God had just called Moses to come up to Him (to climb Mount Sinai). And guess who Moses took with him? He took Joshua. Again we see Moses' commitment to Joshua, and soon we will see the fruit borne from their time together.

In Exodus 24:15-31:18, God gave Moses the Law (and the Ten Commandments— 31:18), along with the instructions for the tabernacle. Then in Exodus 32:1-14, Israel built the golden calf. So here was the situation: Moses had received the Ten Commandments, and it was time to return to the camp. Joshua heard a sound from the camp—a sound that, to him, resembled the sound of war (v. 17). These events caused Moses to interpret what Joshua had heard (v. 18), which exemplifies one of the main purposes of discipleship. We must help those we are discipling to hear correctly. I use "help" because some have abused discipleship and used it as a tool to totally control those they are teaching—to tell them every move to make. This behavior is sin, and God's chastening always rests upon those who choose to respond in such a manner.

Discipleship is not an impossible task. It is being yourself and letting the Lord, who lives in you, rub off on those around you. Simple!

Moses mentions the tent of meeting in Exodus 33:7-11. It was pitched outside the camp, and everyone who sought the Lord would go there. When Moses entered this tent, the glory of the Lord would descend and stand at its entrance, after which the Lord would speak with Moses. When this glory descended, the people would stand and worship at the entrance of their tents. When Moses would depart, Joshua, instead of leaving with Moses, would remain in the tent. Amazing! He had learned from Moses that the most enjoyable thing in life is to sit in God's presence and enjoy Him—all alone, totally alone, with Him. This sitting is why Joshua became a man of God and was used mightily to defeat the Lord's enemies. The time that Joshua spent in the Lord's presence paid high dividends. Just wait and see!!

After Israel departed from Mount Sinai, the people traveled north to the border of Canaan. Before crossing the border, they sent twelve men to spy out the land (Numbers 13:1-16). All of these men, outside of Caleb and Joshua, returned with an unfavorable report (Numbers 13:25-33, 14:1-10). Here is the fruit of discipleship.

Joshua's perspective of the land was totally different from that of those who traveled with him (besides Caleb) because he saw the land through God's eyes. The other men viewed Canaan strictly from the world's vantage point and thus were frightened beyond belief. Joshua, however, knew that the land was God's gift to Israel. No giant, nor anything else, could make him believe otherwise. Time alone with God builds God's perspective into the disciple's life.

Numbers 27:12-23 relates how Moses responded after the Lord informed Him of his upcoming death. Rather than grieving or complaining, he asked the Lord to select a capable leader to direct his people. And guess who the Lord selected? He selected the man who had walked intimately with Moses and intimately with the God of Moses. Do you see what took place here? Joshua not only knew the man who had led God's people, but he knew the heart of the God of the people. Therefore he was selected to succeed Moses as the man of the hour. What a comfort this choice must have been to Moses.

Moses gives a series of sermons in Deuteronomy, recapping the forty years of wilderness wanderings. The messages are addressed to the Israelites who would cross the Jordan to possess the land of promise. Joshua is mentioned first in Deuteronomy 1:38, and is referred to as the man who would cause Israel to inherit the land. Moses also mentions that he had promised Joshua success against the kings east of the Jordan (Deuteronomy 3:21). Later, in Deuteronomy 3:28, Moses was to charge, encourage, and strengthen Joshua, which would prepare him to lead the people to inherit the land. The Lord knew that Joshua needed this encouragement from the man who had impacted his life so significantly.

Deuteronomy 31 says much about Joshua. Moses first states that Joshua would lead the people into the land (v. 3). Later, in verses 7-8, he exhorts Joshua to be strong and courageous and to walk without fear. Moses could make such a statement because he knew that the God who had cared for him would also care for Joshua. But as far as I am concerned, Deuteronomy 31:14-22 is one of the most fascinating and informative sections of this entire book. It was time for Moses to die, and Moses was to bring Joshua to the tent of meeting to commission him (v. 14). Moses and Joshua came to the tent (v. 14), and the Lord appeared in the form of glory (v. 15). I find what occurs next the most interesting. Moses had laid down his life for Israel, and the time had come for him to die. But shortly before his death, God revealed to Moses (and to Joshua, for they were standing together when God spoke with Moses) that the people would forsake Him when they entered the land (vv. 16-18). God's judgment and chastening would then rest on His people. Yet God commanded Moses to write a song that would encourage Israel's future generations to return to the Lord once they recognized their need (vv. 19-22).

Every time I read this account I ask the same question: Had I been Moses, would I have viewed my life as a failure, a total washout? The very people I had loved, cherished, encouraged, and taught would eventually worship the gods of Canaan. Would all of my efforts have been for naught? Of course not, for Joshua would have been standing with me; seeing him would have been encouragement enough for me to die in peace. Joshua was the one who encouraged Moses in his last days. The blessing that Moses placed on Israel in Deuteronomy 33 is confirmation enough that Moses died an obedient, fulfilled, and peaceful man.

But, what about Joshua? He was left holding the bag, so to speak. He was required to lead a nation that would eventually rebel against the God who had given them the land. How would he cope? It was easy. He knew, in an intimate way, the God who had called him to serve. This relationship allowed him to view life from God's perspective, which always results in obedience. Also, God had given him the privilege of walking with a man who had a doctorate in the area of pain and suffering. He would not only survive as the people's leader, but also succeed. He poured his life into faithful men, just as his mentor had done with him. Thus he knew that the truth he had learned from Moses would at least be passed to the generation that followed him.

Deuteronomy 34:9 is wonderful! What a statement! "Now Joshua the son of Nun was filled with the spirit of wisdom, for Moses had laid his hands on him; the sons of Israel listened to him and did as the Lord commanded Moses." Do you catch the message in this verse? Joshua possessed wisdom because Moses had laid his hands on him. But what does the phrase "laid his hands on him" mean? Does it refer to a one-time act, or to a process that took place over a long period of time? I personally believe it is the latter, for we know that Moses laid hands on Joshua for several years. Joshua's wisdom originated in an ongoing relationship with Moses, not in a "laying on of hands" ceremony!

God spoke with Joshua after Moses' death and urged him to take the land (Joshua 1:1-18). But verse 8 is the key verse in this section. Without God's Word to draw from, the disciple will lose his authority and wither on the vine. Moses had taught Joshua the importance of sitting with the Lord, and we will watch as God uses Joshua to defeat His enemies. God's Word bears a bountiful harvest when placed in a hungry heart.

After Joshua had brought Israel into the land, the people went to possess their inheritance (Judges 2:6). But look at Judges 2:7. The people served the Lord throughout Joshua's lifetime and all the days of the elders who had been taught (discipled) by Joshua.

When I first read this verse, I asked, "What happened after the elders died who had walked with Joshua?" Judges 2:10-11 answers this question. A generation arose after them who did not know God—who could not have cared less about what God had done for their forefathers. Their hardened hearts brought rebellion and sin (v. 10), the natural byproduct when a nation rejects truth.

What do we learn from today's lesson? Joshua knew God as his own God, not as Moses' God. It is absolutely essential to remember this truth as we pour our lives into others. If those we disciple never know God personally, if they only learn to feed off of our faith, they are sure to crumble in the heat of the battle.

Be encouraged with your progress. We are learning much that the enemy would enjoy keeping from us. Walk on!

The Life of Paul
(A, B, and C)

First Day—*Memorize Philippians 3:7*

1. Paul speaks of himself in Acts 22:1-21, Acts 26:1-23, and Philippians 3:1-16. Read these sections of Scripture and answer the following questions. Was Paul a Jew?

If so, from which tribe?

Where was he raised (find this location on the map titled ***Journeys of Paul's Life)?***

Who taught Paul the Law?

Write down any other information about Paul's early life that captures your attention.

2. Because you have already read Acts 26:1-23, read Acts 26:24 through 27:44 and write down any new insights. Use the maps supplied with the course. Write down any new prayer requests in your prayer journal each day this week. Also list all answered prayer.

Second Day

1. Read Acts 6:1-9:31, which deals with the life of Stephen. You read these chapters two weeks ago in your Scripture assignment, so you should be familiar with them. Stephen is one of the greatest men in the New Testament. Based on Acts 6, give a description of Stephen.

What impresses you most about Stephen's life?

2. What was Stephen's responsibility in the church at Jerusalem?

Do you think it bothered him to have such a "low-class" assignment?

Explain your answer.

Are you surprised that such a spiritual man was selected for such a common task? Why?

What does this positioning teach you?

3. Read Acts 6:15. Had you been a member of the Council, what would you have thought as you observed Stephen's face?

4. Read Acts 28 and Philippians 1. Philippians was written by Paul during his first imprisonment in Rome, which means he wrote it after his three missionary journeys. Record new insights.

Third Day

1. Acts 7:54-60 tells of Stephen's death. Who observed his death?

What do you think Saul (Paul) was thinking as he watched Stephen die?

How would this incident have helped prepare Paul for salvation?

2. Try to relate Stephen's response to your own walk with Christ. How do Hebrews 12:1-3 and 1Peter 3:8-17 tie in with today's questions?

3. Read Philippians 2-4 and record new insights. Locate Philippi on the map.

Fourth Day—*Memorize Philippians 3:8*

1. Read Acts 9:1-9, Acts 22:1-11, and Acts 26:12-18. Was Saul's (Paul's) conversion experience different from yours?

If so, how?

Paul saw a bright light and was struck blind when he was converted. If your experience did not include these events, do you think you got less of Jesus than Paul did?

Explain.

2. Read Galatians 1-3 and record new insights. Paul wrote Galatians, probably after his first missionary journey and shortly before he visited the Jerusalem council in Acts 15. Find Galatia on the map?

Fifth Day

1. Read Acts 8:26-40. How did the Ethiopian eunuch's conversion differ from Paul's conversion?

What can you learn from this?

In Scripture, whose conversion follows the Ethiopian eunuch's conversion (Acts 9:1-9)?

Why would the Lord place these accounts in this order in His Word?

2. Read Ephesians 4:7 and 1Peter 4:10. What do these verses say about spiritual gifts?

Does it comfort you to know that you have a spiritual gift?

Why?

3. Read Galatians 4-6 and record new insights.

Sixth Day

1. Read this week's lesson and write down any new insights below.

2. Read 1Corinthians 1-3. Paul wrote 1Corinthians while he taught at Ephesus during his third missionary journey. Find Corinth on the map. Record any new insights.

The Life of Paul
(A, B, and C)

A. Paul's Early Life

Paul was a Hebrew (a Jew) of the tribe of Benjamin and a Pharisee (Philippians 3:4-5). He was born and raised in Tarsus of Cilicia and studied under Gamaliel (one of the greatest Jewish teachers of his day—Acts 22:3). He was also a natural-born Roman citizen (Acts 22:26-28). He demonstrated his great zeal for his Jewish ancestry by persecuting the church of Jesus Christ. Concerning the Law's righteousness, he was faultless (Philippians 3:6). In everyday language, Paul was a superstar Jew. His life, until the time he met Christ, was devoted to studying the Law and doing everything in his own power to live the life of a Pharisee.

B. What Helped Prepare Paul for Salvation

God truly works in mysterious ways. Paul was a highly disciplined man who fought for what he believed (Acts 8:3). He wanted to please God in every way possible, but he had a problem. He had the same problem that exists in many lives today. He wanted to work his way into a right standing with God rather than accept God's provision by grace through faith. Paul had to learn that God had paved the way to full acceptance into His Kingdom through Jesus Christ. He needed to see that the Kingdom and its power are not attained through good deeds, but rather by faith (Titus 3:5, Romans 1:16-17, Romans 3:19-24). (Good works are the fruit of faith in Christ, but faith must come first.) We will have the privilege of watching as God brings Paul to repentance.

God knew that Paul desired to please Him. Therefore, God allowed Paul to observe the life of Stephen. We will now look at Stephen through the eyes of Scripture and see what made him special.

Stephen is first mentioned in Acts 6, where the disciples are having difficulties with the daily serving of food. The disciples (the twelve) needed to teach the Word instead of wait on tables. As a result, Stephen was selected to wait on tables and serve food in Jerusalem. This task was perhaps lowly, but required men of character. Every man selected was to have a good reputation and be full of the Spirit and wisdom (v. 3).

Stephen was abundantly blessed in both areas. He was filled with the Spirit of God, which gave him power that could only be explained by his relationship with Jesus Christ.

Paul had religion with no power; Stephen had Christ with power galore. Paul had Law with no life; Stephen had the Holy Spirit with life abundant. Paul had nothing but dead works; Stephen had intimacy with the God of the universe. Paul lived a life of duty and despair; Stephen knew Christ's freedom, which filled him to overflowing with peace and joy.

God saw Paul's need to observe the real thing in a real life. Therefore, He allowed Paul to watch as Stephen endured the most trying circumstances imaginable. You can argue doctrine, you can argue theology, you can argue many different things, but you cannot argue a transformed life filled with God's power.

Stephen was full of grace and power and was performing great wonders and signs among the people (Acts 6:8). These acts came as a result of being filled with God's Spirit (Acts 6:3). (We all receive the Holy Spirit at the point of salvation but we must be filled with God's Spirit on a moment-by-moment basis [Ephesians 5:18]. This occurs when we walk in constant, unbroken fellowship with the Lord.) Stephen also spoke with great wisdom (Acts 6:10). He did have his enemies; they took him before the Council (the Sanhedrin [Acts 6:11-14]). Considering Stephen's circumstances, it would seem that he had every right to panic. But Acts 6:15 states that his face was like that of an angel— in other words, he was resting in the Lord's ability to meet his needs. The council witnessed his peace in the midst of the storm. However, after listening to Stephen's sermon (Acts 7:1-53), they did what most people do whose theology has been discredited. They decided to eliminate the source of the conflict. (Don't most people whose theology has been discredited either ignore or discredit the source that proved them incorrect, rather then allow the truth to set them free?) The Council was furious (v. 54), but Stephen was unaffected because he drew everything he needed from the Father and His Son Jesus Christ (vv. 55-56). Even when they stoned him (v. 59), he asked the Lord not to hold their sin against them (v. 60).

What an example! Anyone who had observed Stephen's death would have been in awe of God's power radiating from his life. And guess who was one of the spectators? You guessed it—Paul (Acts 7:58, 8:1). I truly believe it was Stephen who prepared Paul for salvation. Although Paul persecuted the church even after Stephen's death (Acts 8:3), he soon came to know Christ.

C. Paul's Salvation Experience

Acts 9:1-9, Acts 22:1-11 and Acts 26:12-18 relate the details of Paul's conversion. Some are tempted to say one of two things after reading these passages. The first is, "My salvation experience didn't include being struck blind, so maybe it didn't take." The second is, "If Jesus appeared to me, then I, like Paul, could become a great disciple."

One of the first things the disciple must learn is that everyone's salvation experience is different. We all receive the same Jesus, but the events surrounding His coming vary widely. Compare Paul's conversion with the Ethiopian eunuch's in Acts 8:26-40. Was the eunuch struck blind? Of course not, but he received the same Jesus that Paul would later receive. Notice the order of events in Acts 8 and 9. When the Lord finished the account of the Ethiopian eunuch (Acts 8:26-40), what did he record next? You guessed it! He recorded the account of Paul's conversion.

I believe these events are placed in this order for a specific reason. I sense the Lord is saying, "When I come into lives, I have a very profound and lasting effect, but every person's experience is different." I know my own experience did not include a bolt of lightning—not even a fuzzy feeling. In fact, very little took place emotionally, but I did receive peace. Your experience might have been just the opposite, and that's wonderful. My point is that no matter what happened to your feeler (emotions), if you repented and in faith asked Christ into your life, then rest assured that He came in and made you a new creation (2Corinthians 5:17).

Satan has tricked many into believing their salvation experience was not real. If you have repented of your sins and asked Christ to be Lord of your life, then you have been born again, no matter what events took place at the time. Rest in the knowledge, that He has everything under control.

We may also find ourselves saying, "If I had a gift like Paul's, then I could do what Paul did for the Kingdom." Two things are wrong with this attitude. First, Scripture teaches that all believers receive a spiritual gift (Ephesians 4:7, 1Peter 4:10). God gave you your particular gift at the point of salvation, but it is manifested with boldness only as you mature in your walk with Christ. I repeat; God has given you a spiritual gift! This truth is concrete, so accept it and press on. All you need to do now is learn how to use what God has given you. Second, we must learn, as Paul did, that we can do nothing "for" the Kingdom, but Christ "through us" can do all things. We will soon observe how Paul learned this great truth.

In next week's study we will learn how Paul became a disciple. It should be fun!

The Life of Paul
(D, 1, 2, and 3)

First Day—*Memorize 2Timothy 3:12*

1. Read Acts 9:8-22. What kept Paul from walking into Damascus on his own?

How did he find his way to Damascus?

What does his experience say about the importance of having someone to assist us when we first become believers?

2. Who was Ananias?

Why was he reluctant to visit Paul?

How would you have felt had you been Ananias?

When was the last time the Lord asked you to do something that looked "risky"?

How did you respond?

Are you facing a risky situation today?

What must you do to view it as an opportunity?

3. Read 1Corinthians 4-6 and record new insights. Write down any new prayer requests in your prayer journal each day this week. Also list all answered prayers.

Second Day

1. Read Acts 9:15. Would you like to bear the name of the Lord before the Gentiles and kings and the sons of Israel?

Now read Acts 9:16. Do you still want to do so?

Read 2Corinthians 11:16-12:10 to bring all of these thoughts into focus. What is the Lord showing you about the cost of leadership and discipleship?

2. How does the previous question tie in with Matthew 10:34-39 and John 16:1-3, 33?

3. Read 1Corinthians 7-9 and record new insights.

Third Day—*Memorize Ephesians 5:18*

1. Read Acts 9:17 and Ephesians 5:18. What does it mean to be "filled with the Holy Spirit"?

Also read Acts 13:9. Can this filling occur over and over in our lives?
If so, how?

Why would Paul need to be filled with the Holy Spirit?

What happened to Paul when this filling occurred (Acts 9:18)?

What does his experience communicate to you?

2. What was Paul's topic as he preached in Damascus (vv. 19-22)?

List some verses that Paul could have used to preach on this topic?

3. Read 1Corinthians 10-11 and record new insights.

Fourth Day

1. From Acts 9:21, why were the people so amazed at Paul? (Hint: Was it his message, or his change of lifestyle, or both that amazed his listeners?)

2. Read Acts 9:22. Do you think Paul spoke this message in love?

Explain.

Read Acts 9:20-22. How many came to the Lord as a result of Paul's preaching?

3. Read 1Corinthians 12-14. Record any new insights.

Fifth Day—*Memorize John 8:31-32*

1. Acts 9:23 includes: "And when many days elapsed." Where do you think Paul spent these many days? For help, read Galatians 1:15-17.

Why would the Lord decide for Paul to leave Damascus and move to Arabia?

2. Where did Paul go after he left Arabia?

What happened to him once he arrived (Galatians 1:15-17, Acts 9:23-25)?

3. Read 1Corinthians 15-16 and record new insights.

Sixth Day

1. Does any Scripture, besides Acts 9:25, refer to Paul's "basket case" experience? You may need to use a concordance to find your answer. (Note: If you do not have an exhaustive concordance, you should make every effort to obtain one as soon as possible. They are very helpful, and most Christian bookstores carry them. There are online resources available as well.)

2. What might Paul have been thinking as they lowered him over the wall?

Have you ever had a similar experience?

If so, write it down and be prepared to share it with your small group.

3. Read this week's lesson and record any new insights.

4. Read 2Corinthians 1-4. Paul wrote this epistle from Macedonia while on his third missionary journey. Record any new insights in your notebook.

The Life of Paul
(D, 1, 2, and 3)

D. How Paul Became a Disciple

One of the most interesting things we could research is how Paul became a disciple. Many feel that Paul's Damascus road experience prepared him instantly for ministry. However, a large span of time elapsed between that experience and the time he was ready for service. He was equipped with everything he needed when he met Christ, but several years passed before he could use what he had received for the glory of Christ.

Like most of us, Paul had to learn the hard but essential lesson that he was powerless. Paul had been educated in the Law (Mosaic Law—the Law given to Moses on Mt. Sinai), he knew the Old Testament like the back of his hand, and he had seen Jesus on the Damascus road. But he had not yet learned to express what he knew "in love." I believe Paul's early messages were 100 percent correct doctrinally. I say this because of Acts 9:22, where Paul proves that Jesus was the Christ. The only way he could have proven Jesus' Messiahship was by referring to Old Testament Scripture. However, I sense that much of what he said was brutal (truth without love is brutality). Please don't misunderstand me. Paul did exactly what he felt he should do but lacked the maturity to approach his calling from God's perspective. He did not yet understand that God wanted to do the work through him—not him for God.

I truly appreciate this portion of Paul's life. It illustrates that we must be broken before God can use us. Seven topics are listed under Section III, Part D of your outline; all seven are very useful and informative.

1. Paul's Time in Damascus (Acts 9:8-22)

This segment of Paul's life is addressed in Acts 9:8-22. Paul's traveling companions had brought him to Damascus (v. 8) when the Lord advised Ananias to visit him (vv. 10-12). Ananias was to lay his hands on Paul, at which time Paul would regain his sight (v. 12). This task must have been very trying for Ananias (Acts 9:13-14). God's statements in verses 15 and 16 teach us much about the results and cost of discipleship. Most of us want results without cost. However, God's Kingdom doesn't work that way. It never has and it never will. We would all like to "bear" God's name before the Gentiles and kings and the sons of Israel (v. 15), but we cringe when we think of the suffering we might face as a result of it or in preparation for it (v. 16).

As we observe God's power in Paul's life, remember that it came as a result of brokenness—which came as a result of suffering. Pain was a vital part of what made him into a man of God (read 2Corinthians 11:23-29). We will also suffer, but the good news is that God's grace is sufficient

In Acts 9:17-19, Ananias visits Paul, at which time Paul was filled with the Holy Spirit. Every believer is filled with the Holy Spirit at the point of salvation, and this filling can and should occur over and over in the believer's life (Ephesians 5:18). We'll discuss this later in more detail.

Paul's sight was restored, and he spent much time with the disciples in Damascus (vv. 18-19). But watch what followed: Paul immediately started preaching Jesus in the synagogue while his listeners stood amazed (vv. 20-21). But why were they amazed?

This is so very important—please don't miss this point! Scripture doesn't indicate whether anyone was saved through Paul's preaching (Acts 9:20-22). I believe the amazement resulted, not from the content of Paul's message, but from his change of lifestyle. Read verse 21 again and you will see my point. Not one comment addresses what Paul had said, but his change of lifestyle had truly astounded them. Isn't this the way it is when we first come to Christ? People are amazed at our change of lifestyle, but we must write His Word on our hearts before we can speak with both authority and compassion. We want to preach, but the Lord says, "Sit with Me and let Me show you My heart." Remember what Paul wrote to Timothy in 1Timothy 3:6? He realized from his own experience that new converts have no business leading the local church!

Look again at verse 22. *"But Saul kept increasing in strength and confounding the Jews who lived at Damascus by proving that this Jesus is the Christ." "Confounding"* means to bewilder in the form of a quarrel or dispute. How much of Paul's message do you think was spoken in "agape" love? Also note the word *"proving."*

Paul had to "prove" his point, and his listeners must have sensed this need in his message. Paul was like a bull in a china shop. All he saw was red!

From our study of the life of Moses, what was the remedy to Paul's problem? You guessed it. He needed a healthy dose of stillness before his God. He needed a prolonged period of time to do nothing but sit and bask in the radiance of His presence. After all, it was the only means through which Paul would take on His character (2Corinthians 3:18). Paul was now ready for Arabia!

2. Paul's Time in Arabia (Acts 9:23a, Galatians 1:11-17)

Arabia was relatively close to Damascus (look at the map *Journeys of Paul's Early Life)*. Because it was desolate, it was an ideal location to sit with God. (Remember how Moses sat alone in Midian as a shepherd.) Scripture doesn't say much about this segment of Paul's life, but Galatians 1:15-17 does state that he spent time in Arabia. While there, he sat alone with God, for verses 16-17 reveal that he did not consult with flesh and blood. Many days elapsed between the time he initially preached in Damascus (Acts 9:20-22) and his return from Arabia (Acts 9:23). (He could have spent as much as three years in Arabia, but we can't be certain.) Our concern is not the amount of time, but rather that he went to be alone with the Lord. Oh, how we need to see the importance of this time for our lives!

3. Paul's Time in Damascus (Acts 9:23-25, Galatians 1:17b)

I have often wondered what was going on in Paul's mind as he traveled from Arabia to Damascus. He had "sat" for quite some time, but he was still only a maximum of four years old in the Lord. A great possibility exists that he felt he had all the training needed to "win the world for Christ." But we will soon find that his training had just begun. What he experienced when he returned to Damascus had a lasting impact on the remainder of his life.

Paul returned (Galatians 1:17), but instead of finding that revival had broken out as a result of his initial visit, he received persecution from those to whom he had preached. The persecution became so severe that he was lowered in a basket through an opening in the city wall (Acts 9:23-25, 2Corinthians 11:32-33). Paul literally was a "basket case." Don't you know this experience was painful to endure! But oh, the sovereignty of God! God would use this to teach Paul humility, a much-needed ingredient for those who want to live on the cutting edge of God's economy (James 4:6).

Paul's disciples lowered him over the wall (Acts 9:25). These men might have been believers, but we can't be certain. The word "disciple" in Scripture does not always refer to "true believers" (John 6:60-71). These "disciples" at Damascus could have been men who were learning truth, but who had not made a commitment to Christ. The reason I say this is that I truly believe Paul's first convert was Sergius Paulus, a man mentioned in Acts 13. We will discuss this man in more detail later in the course.

You are doing great! Isn't this fun?

The Life of Paul
(D, 4, 5, 6, and 7)

First Day—*Memorize John 1:12*

1. Where did Paul go after he left Damascus (Acts 9:26-29)?

How was he received?

How would you have felt had you been Paul?

2. Who befriended Paul in Jerusalem?

What was the meaning of this person's name (Acts 4:36)?

Do you have a Barnabas to go to when you need encouragement?

Who is that person?

Do you consider yourself to be a Barnabas?

If not, what changes need to take place for you to become such a person?

For motivation, read through Colossians 4:7-8, 1Thessalonians 3:2, 1Thessalonians 5:11, 1Thessalonians 5:14, Titus 2:3-4, and Hebrews 3:13.

3. Read 2Corinthians 5-7 and record new insights. Write down any new prayer requests in your prayer journal, each day this week. Also list all answered prayer.

Second Day

1. Read Acts 9:26-39. Why would the Hellenistic Jews in Jerusalem react to Paul in such a manner?

What did they try to do to him?

Can you relate to what happened in these verses?

If so, how?

2. Where was Paul sent next (v. 30)?

Find these locations on the map. What was Tarsus to Paul (Acts 22:3)?

3. Read Acts 9:31. What happened to the church throughout Judea, Galilee, and Samaria after Paul departed?

What conclusions do you draw from this situation?

4. When did God last place you on a shelf and reduce your activity to draw you closer to Himself?

What did you learn from the experience?

After studying Paul's life, how will you react if God chooses to do it again?

5. Read 2 Corinthians 8-10 and record new insights.

Third Day—*Memorize John 14:6*

1. Read Acts 11:19-26. (You may want to read Acts 9:32-11:18 to bring yourself up to date.) Find Antioch on the map. How did the Greeks in Antioch hear the news about Jesus?

How was Stephen connected?

What does this situation tell you about the sovereignty of God (and Romans 8:28)?

2. Why was it big news in Jerusalem when the Greeks in Antioch believed?

How did the church at Jerusalem respond when they heard this news (v. 22)?

Had you been Barnabas, what thoughts would have crossed your mind as you traveled to Antioch? (He would be visiting not just Jewish converts but also Gentiles.)

3. Read Acts 11:23. Try to relate to what Barnabas experienced here. How would you have responded?

From verse 23, what did Barnabas do that allowed him to live up to his name?

4. Read 2Corinthians 11-13 and record new insights.

Fourth Day

1. Read Acts 11:19-26. How is Barnabas described in Acts 11:24?

From our previous lessons, what does it mean to be full of the Holy Spirit?

Where did Barnabas go when he departed from Antioch (v. 25)?

Who was staying there whom Barnabas would have been interested in seeing?

Why was Barnabas sent to Paul at this time?

2. Where did Barnabas initially take Paul (v. 26)?

What did they do there and how long did they stay?

3. God sent Barnabas to Paul only after Paul was useful for service. What does this timing say to you about your own life?

4. Why would God allow an influential man such as Paul to spend so much time away from mainstream Christian activity?

How did God respond when Paul was equipped for ministry?

Did Paul open the door of ministry for himself, or did he allow the Lord to open it for him? Write down your thoughts below.

5. What was the most meaningful thing you learned from this portion of the course?

What have you learned about the importance of spending time alone with the Lord?

6. Read 1Peter 1-2 and record new insights. Peter wrote this epistle. Next week, in Acts 15, you will read about Peter, Paul, and Barnabas as they met with the Jerusalem council. Thus, read 1Peter and 2Peter this week rather than later.

Fifth Day—*Memorize Ephesians 2:8*
1. According to Acts 11:27-30, why did Paul and Barnabas travel to Jerusalem?

What does verse 29 say to you about the importance of helping the needy?

2. Read Acts 12:1-25. How was Herod responding to the believers in Jerusalem around the time that Paul and Barnabas were there?

Who returned to Antioch with them (v. 25)?

3. Read 1Peter 3-5. Record new insights.

Sixth Day

1. Read this week's lesson and record any new insights.

2. Read 2Peter 1-3 and record new insights.

The Life of Paul
(D, 4, 5, 6, and 7)

D. How Paul Became a Disciple

4. Paul's Time in Jerusalem (Acts 9:26-29)

After Paul's "basket case" experience in Damascus, he came to Jerusalem (Acts 9:26-29). While there he tried to associate with his fellow believers, but they were afraid of him (v. 26). Can you imagine how he must have felt? Not only had the Jews in Damascus attempted to kill him, but now the Jews in Jerusalem were also questioning the legitimacy of his salvation. Barnabas had to convince the apostles that Paul was a genuine believer (v. 27).

After studying Paul's life, is it any wonder that the Lord encourages us to fix our eyes on Jesus (Hebrews 12:2)? Only when we consider Christ's sufferings (Hebrews 12:3) are we capable of viewing our circumstances from God's vantage point. The Lord tells us not to be surprised at the testing we face as believers, not to think of it as though some strange thing were happening (1Peter 4:12). He urges us to rejoice even when things look impossible (1Peter 4:13). Can you see why we must know Christ as our life? We must never be satisfied with knowing Him only as Savior!

After Barnabas had verified Paul's legitimacy, Paul spoke out boldly in Jerusalem (v. 28). But instead of speaking the truth in love, he argued with those who sat under his teaching (Acts 9:29). Thus, the Jews attempted to put him to death. It is hard to believe that their cause for irritation was solely the content of Paul's message. I believe that many of the hardships of Paul's early ministry resulted from his lack of love and concern for his listeners. Paul had much to learn, so the Lord allowed him to withdraw to Tarsus to take on more of His character (Acts 9:29-30, 2Corinthians 3:18).

I hope you don't hear me saying that a Christian cannot stand boldly for what he or she believes. We should oppose anything that is not of God, but we must be careful to do so in the spirit of love and self-control (Galatians 5:22-23). Paul himself stated that we are to do all things without grumbling or disputing so we may prove ourselves to be blameless and innocent (Philippians 2:14-15). Here, Paul was encouraging believers to refrain from arguing among themselves, but we can also apply this advice to our relationships with non-believers. One of the first lessons we must learn is that we don't acquire (or master) Scripture to argue Scripture.

Later in his life, Paul stated, "The Lord's bondservant must not be quarrelsome, but be kind to all, able to teach, patient when wronged, with gentleness correcting those who are in opposition" (2Timothy 2:24-25). Paul's attitudes had changed concerning how to present God's truth. He was now mature in the Lord, which caused him to realize his need to present what he knew in gentleness. By no means did Paul compromise his message. Please do not read that into these verses! Paul had learned how to love during his walk with the Lord, and it totally transformed the way he communicated the gospel that had become so dear to him. However, he never once compromised when presenting this gospel to those who so desperately needed it.

5. Paul's Time in Tarsus (Acts 9:30-31)

The believers in Jerusalem sent Paul to Tarsus (Acts 9:30). But you may ask, "What happened to the church in Jerusalem and the surrounding areas after Paul's departure? Could it possibly survive?" You bet it could! It not only survived, but it also enjoyed peace and continued growth (Acts 9:31).

Some of us think the Christian community would fold if we were not at every meeting, potluck dinner, work day—practically every function of the community or church. Paul may have felt the same way, but obviously the church managed quite well without him. Time alone with Christ will more than compensate for anything we might miss during our time away. Having His Word fresh on our hearts makes us fountains from which others can drink, instead of half empty cups of the world's rubble!

Are you beginning to see the big picture? Is it becoming obvious that we must eliminate some of our doing and start learning to be? Sitting allows us to learn what God has accomplished for us through Christ. Here we learn about rest and how we are to allow Jesus' life to work through us—not us working for Him. Lasting fruit will then be borne from our activity, fruit that will endure throughout eternity!

One word of warning: If you don't want to be used of the Lord, don't start "sitting" with Him. Those equipped with His Word find themselves walking through doors they never dreamed existed. Let's now watch as the Lord opens a wide door of effective ministry for the apostle Paul.

6. Paul's Time in Antioch (Acts 11:19-26)

Paul had been sitting with the Lord for several years (he could have been in Tarsus for as long as 13 or 14 years), but now he was ready for ministry. Could you have waited the length of time that Paul waited? Let's watch as the Lord confirms that the time had come for him to start his public ministry.

An interesting thing had happened in Antioch. Men from Cyprus and Cyrene had traveled to Antioch and preached Jesus to the Greeks there. Many of these Greeks believed (Acts 11:19-21). When the church at Jerusalem received word of their conversion, they sent Barnabas to Antioch (Acts 11:22). Remember Barnabas from Acts 9:27? Isn't the sovereignty of God remarkable! The church at Jerusalem could have sent any number of people, but they "happened" to choose Barnabas. And guess what Barnabas did when he arrived in Antioch? After he visited the people, he left for Tarsus to look for Paul (Acts 11:23-25).

Now that Paul was equipped for ministry, nothing—absolutely nothing—would stop him. Paul was not asked to open a single door of ministry. They were opened for him! Paul's ministry had been prepared by God (Acts 11:26), and the Lord continued to open doors for him for the rest of his life.

7. Paul's Time in Jerusalem (Acts 11:27-30, 12:1-25)

The disciples sent Paul and Barnabas from Antioch with a contribution to the believers in Judea (Acts 11:27-30). Acts 12 points out that much persecution was directed toward the church at Jerusalem during this general time period. Herod killed James, the brother of John (v. 2). Herod also had Peter cast into prison (v. 3). Such persecution could have discouraged Paul and Barnabas, but they remained true to the faith and fulfilled their mission (v. 25).

John Mark returned to Antioch with Paul and Barnabas. John Mark would travel with Paul in the beginning stages of his first missionary journey. We will deal more with his life in next week's material.

Is the Lord turning on some lights for you? Are you starting to see how God transforms ordinary people into disciples? Isn't this exciting? Let's get to the task before us!

The Life of Paul
(E, 1)

First Day

1. Read Acts 13-14. As you read these two chapters, use the maps located in the back of the book. Write down any new insights.

2. Read Colossians 1-4 and record new insights. Paul wrote this epistle during his first imprisonment in Rome after he had made his three missionary journeys. He had never visited this church. Find Colossae on the map. Write down any new prayer requests in your prayer journal each day this week. Also list any answered prayer.

Second Day

1. Read Acts 13:1-12. Who was converted to Christ on the island of Cyprus?

Why was this conversion so meaningful to Paul? (For help in answering this question, try to find a place where Paul had previously led someone to Christ, if such a place exists.)

2. Read Acts 13:13. Why would John Mark choose to go home?

How would you have responded to John Mark had you been Paul?

How did you respond to the last person who severed a relationship with you because of a difference of opinion?

Are you doing all you can to resolve the conflict?

If so, what is it you are doing?

3. Read 1Thessalonians 1-4. Paul wrote this epistle from Corinth while on his second missionary journey. Find Thessalonica on the map. Record new insights.

Third Day—*Memorize Colossians 1:13*

1. (Challenge question) Where was John Mark from and who won him to the Lord? You may need to call some of your group members for assistance.

2. Read Colossians 4:10. How was John Mark related to Barnabas?

3. What book in the New Testament did John Mark write?

Where did you get your information?

4. Read 1Thessalonians 5 and 2Thessalonians 1-3. Paul wrote 2Thessalonians on his second missionary journey while still at Corinth a short time after he wrote 1Thessalonians. Record new insights.

Fourth Day

1. Read Acts 13:13-52. Why did Paul visit the synagogue?

2. What impressed you the most about Paul's sermon in Acts 13:16-41?

What do verses 38 and 39 say to you?

3. Why did the Jews oppose what Paul and Barnabas were teaching (Acts 13:44-45)?

What does this opposition tell you about the importance of removing all jealousy from our lives?

How does Acts 13:46 tie in with the last phrase of Romans 1:16?

4. What does Acts 13:52 communicate to you?

Can this same joy and power exist in your life?

Do you consider yourself to be a joyful person?

If not, what must occur before you can possess this joy (Galatians 5:22)?

5. Read Titus 1-3 and Philemon. After Paul's first imprisonment in Rome, he was released for a time, and then imprisoned again (in Rome). Between his first and second imprisonments, he established a church in Crete. Paul placed Titus in charge of this church (Titus 1:5), which is why Paul corresponded with him. Paul also wrote Philemon during his first imprisonment in Rome. Record your new insights.

Fifth Day—*Memorize Romans 8:1*

1. Read Acts 14:1-28. Where did Paul preach in Iconium (v. 1)?

Again, how does this location tie in with the last phrase of Romans 1:16?

What caused Paul and his companions to leave Iconium?

2. What does Acts 14:8-18 tell you about Paul's character and his desire to glorify God?

3. What happened to Paul in Acts 14:19?

According to 2Timothy 3:10-11, who was observing Paul's life as Paul experienced these persecutions?

What effect do you think these observations had on Timothy?

4. Did Paul return to Lystra?

If so, for what purpose?

Read Acts 14:22-23 and write down your thoughts as you observe Paul's desire to teach and encourage those who had come to know Christ. Have you yet realized that, "Through many tribulations we must enter the kingdom of God" (v. 22)?

Does this knowledge encourage or discourage you?

5. Read Hebrews 1-4 and record new insights. It is uncertain as to who wrote Hebrews, but it is a wonderful book. In fact, Hebrews and Romans may very well be the most important books in the New Testament. Hebrews meshes well with Paul's writings.

Sixth Day

1. Read Acts 14:24-28. Be sure to use the maps. Record your new insights.

2. Read Acts 14:27 and imagine that you were Paul. What would you have reported first? (Wouldn't it have been exciting to have been there!)

3. What does Acts 14:28 tell you about the importance of sharing what God is doing in our lives with those we have come to know and love in the Lord Jesus? They spent a "long" time with those with whom they shared. What changes are you making to allow yourself quality time with those interested in knowing the heart of Christ?

4. Read this week's lesson and record new insights.

5. Read Hebrews 5-7. Record any new insights.

The Life of Paul
(E, 1)

E. Paul's Life as a Disciple

1. Paul's First Missionary Journey and First Convert (Acts 13-14)

The Holy Spirit instructed the church at Antioch to send Paul and Barnabas to the work in which they were called (Acts 13:1-3). After they received the church's blessings, Paul and Barnabas (v. 4) took John Mark (v. 5) and sailed to Cyprus. We must examine closely their stay at Paphos of Cyprus or we might overlook something very significant. To this point, Paul has been referred to as Saul. Only after he leaves Cyprus is he called Paul (Acts 13:13). An extraordinary event occurred there that totally revolutionized Paul's life and propelled him to new heights in his walk with Christ.

In Acts 13:7 a man named Sergius Paulus comes on the scene. Verses 7-12 tell that he was the proconsul and a very intelligent man. What we have learned so far allows us to dig deeper as we examine these verses. Nowhere have we read of anyone coming to Christ through Paul's ministry. We have read a great deal about Paul's preaching, but nothing about any conversions.

Guess what happened at Paphos of Cyprus? Sergius Paulus believed (v. 12). Did you hear that? Sergius Paulus believed! I personally view this event as not only revolutionizing Sergius Paulus' life, but also Paul's life. At last God used Paul to lead someone to Christ, an event that moved him so much that he was never the same. It touched him so deeply that verse 13 refers to him as "Paul" instead of "Saul." The fact that Paul wanted to remember Sergius Paulus probably had much to do with the changing of his name.

Have you wondered how Paul remained encouraged in the midst of his numerous trials (2Corinthians 11:23-33)? I believe he overcame by saying, "Jesus, I can do all things through Your power, for You live in me. And Lord, I remember the awesome impact You had on the life of Sergius Paulus. I will continue in Your strength regardless of the degree of pain or hardship I might endure." Paul had seen the Lord transform a life before his very eyes, and he never got over it.

Have you had the opportunity to pray with someone to receive Christ? If so, you know it is an awesome experience that leaves you changed forever. Isn't it encouraging when the Lord uses us to minister to the needs of others? As far as I'm concerned that experience is heaven on earth. Paul tasted that kind of joy at Paphos of Cyprus, and that sample motivated him to new heights of service.

After Paul, Barnabas, and John Mark departed from Paphos, they arrived in Perga. Here John Mark left them and returned to Jerusalem (Acts 13:13). We can learn much about discipleship from the life of John Mark. Scripture doesn't state why he left, but Acts 15:36-40 reveals that Paul was not pleased with John Mark's decision. On the surface it might appear that John Mark was simply too "tender" to finish the journey. His family owned servants and a home that was large enough to hold prayer meetings for many of the saints at Jerusalem (Acts 12:12-14). He was also a cousin to Barnabas (Colossians 4:10), who was himself wealthy (Acts 4:36-37). Therefore, John Mark probably came from an affluent background in which life was relatively easy. Even so, I doubt that his upbringing explains his departure.

Maybe he was just too immature for such an undertaking. I seriously doubt this reason, however, since Peter had won him to the Lord (1Peter 5:13). He also had many opportunities while in Jerusalem to learn from some of the great men of the faith, for his mother's home was a meeting place for Christians (Acts 12:12). I am certain that our answer lies deeper.

To find a possible explanation for his leaving, we must examine the meaning of his name. John is his Hebrew name and Mark his Roman name. Now look at Acts 13:5 and 13. How is John Mark referred to in these two passages? He is called John in both instances—his Hebrew name! There are hints that his family, like Paul's, followed the Hebrew tradition to the letter. I think a possible explanation for his leaving is that he objected to Paul's offer of salvation to the Gentiles on the basis of faith alone. I believe that when John Mark saw Sergius Paulus, a Roman, accept Paul's offer of salvation through faith, it was more than he could handle. So he packed his bags and went home. At this time Paul almost stood by himself in his conviction concerning the Gentiles' salvation through repentance and faith alone. In fact, Barnabas still had misgivings even later (Galatians 2:11-21).

Look again at Acts 15:36-39. John Mark is called Mark. I think his attitude had changed concerning Gentile salvation through faith. Therefore, he was called by his Roman name (Mark). He wanted to join Paul on Paul's second journey, so we can assume that he finally agreed with Paul's message. But because he had failed to complete the first journey (v. 38), Paul had misgivings. Their relationship was restored later, for Mark was with Paul during his first imprisonment in Rome (Colossians 4:10 and Philemon 24). However, for the time being Paul made a tough choice and left Mark behind.

A disciple must know that salvation is based on faith, not faith plus works. Works will follow salvation, but they do not save the believer. It is repentance and faith that brings new birth. Mark eventually recognized this truth and became very useful to Paul in the ministry. He even wrote the Gospel of Mark.

Are you following Paul's travels on the map titled *Paul's First Missionary Journey?*

After John Mark left, Paul and Barnabas traveled from Perga to Pisidian Antioch where they preached and taught in the synagogue (Acts 13:14-52). Have you noticed that when Paul entered a new city he would preach in the synagogue first? He believed that the gospel should be presented to the Jew first and then to the Greek (Romans 1:16).

Verses 38-39 (of Acts 13) are powerful; for they settle the issue that faith in Christ frees us from all things from which we could not be freed while living under Law. Still, many of the Jews rejected Paul's message of freedom by grace through faith. Those who did so became very jealous when they realized that many were listening to Paul's message (v. 45). As a result, they tried to contradict what Paul had been teaching (v. 45), but many came to Christ in Pisidian Antioch, and God was greatly glorified (vv. 46-49). Paul and Barnabas were severely persecuted, but verse 52 states, "And the disciples were continually filled with joy and with the Holy Spirit." There is peace in the midst of the storm. Thank you Jesus!

Paul and Barnabas then traveled to Iconium and taught in the synagogue (Acts 14:16). But when their lives were threatened they moved to Lystra (v. 6). Something followed that is a great object lesson for those who are becoming disciples. First, the miracles that God performed through Paul were misunderstood. Thus the people wanted to worship Paul and Barnabas instead of the God of Paul and Barnabas (vv. 8-18). This naturally upset Paul and Barnabas, for they had done everything possible to point their listeners to Christ. This example confirms that what we teach and do can many times be totally misinterpreted by those who observe our lives. Don't forget what you have learned here. It will be of great value as you mature in the faith.

Paul was later stoned in Lystra and left for dead outside the city (v.19). Had you been Paul, how would you have responded to this series of events? Do you think the Lord could possibly use all of this misfortune for good? You bet He could, for a young man named Timothy saw Paul's sufferings firsthand (2Timothy 3:10-11). And what did Timothy see in Paul? He saw a power that could only be explained in terms of Jesus Christ. I am sure that Timothy had never seen a man who was willing to die for the gospel. Possibly he had heard rumors about this Christ, but now he had witnessed His power firsthand. We know that Timothy was converted under Paul's ministry, for Paul refers to him as his beloved son (1Corinthians 4:17, 1Timothy 1:2, and 2Timothy 1:2). Paul also discipled Timothy.

Paul does an amazing thing in verse 20. After being stoned, he returns to Lystra. Can you believe he would do such a thing? Talk about boldness! The next day, however, he and Barnabas traveled to Derbe (v. 20) and then returned back through Lystra, Iconium, and Antioch strengthening the disciples and appointing elders in every church (vv. 21-23). Can you imagine Timothy's feelings as he watched Paul pass through Lystra a third time? (Some believe that Paul had the experience described in 2Corinthians 12:1-4 when he was stoned in Lystra and left for dead outside the city.)

From Pisidian Antioch Paul and Barnabas traveled to Perga and Attalia and eventually sailed back to Antioch in Syria (vv. 24-28). (Are you following all of this on the map? Did you note the different locations of the two Antiochs?) Can you imagine what the disciples reported to the church in Antioch? They could have told "war stories" for days. I am sure we would have enjoyed being a fly on the wall. Someday, however, we will have the awesome privilege of speaking with Paul face to face. I want him to tell me the one about Lystra.

Are you starting to see how the Lord uses a disciple to draw others to Himself? Through the problems Paul endured, the Lord touched Timothy! As we become disciples, the Lord will touch those around us as they watch us face life's many difficulties. They, like Timothy, will want to know our Jesus. And guess what? We will be equipped to tell them all about Him. Isn't that neat?

You are doing great, and you will be doing even better after you study Paul's second missionary journey, the main topic in next week's material.

The Life of Paul
(E, 2, 3, and 4)

First Day-*Memorize Jude 24*

1. Read Acts 15:1-29. Follow along on the maps. Paul and Barnabas traveled to Jerusalem before Paul embarked on his second missionary journey. For what purpose did they travel to Jerusalem?

Whom did they meet with when they arrived?

Who seems to be the leader of the church in Jerusalem (v.13, Acts 12:17, Galatians 2:9, 12)?

2. What impressed you about the way Peter, Paul, and Barnabas handled the situation in Jerusalem?

Did their experience with the Gentiles influence the council's decision?

Those who have been in battle, and who know the price of discipleship, carry the greatest impact when it comes to decision-making.

Do you have mature people around you to help you make the tough decisions?

If so, who are they?

3. Read Hebrews 8-9. Record your new insights. Write down any new prayer requests in your prayer journal each day this week. Also list all answered prayer.

Second Day

1. Read Acts 15:30-35. Who traveled to Antioch with Paul and Barnabas?

What did Paul and Barnabas do when they arrived in Antioch?

What did the two men from Jerusalem do in Antioch?

Which one chose to remain in Antioch?

2. Read Acts 15:36-41. Why did Paul and Barnabas go their separate ways?

Whom did Barnabas take with him and where did they go?

Why would they go there?

3. Who traveled with Paul on his second missionary journey?

Considering what you learned earlier, how had they become acquainted?

What did you learn about this man from Acts 15:22?

Does this event explain why Paul would want him along on his second missionary journey?

4. Read Hebrews 10-11 and record new insights.

THIRD DAY—*Memorize Hebrews 10:14*

1. Read Acts 15:36-16:5. How do you think Paul felt as he departed on his second journey? (Remember what had taken place between Paul and Barnabas.)

How do disagreements with other believers affect you?

How do you go about reconciling those disagreements?

When God is preparing to bless you, what normally precedes that blessing?

2. Whom did Paul invite to join him and Silas in Lystra?

What did Paul do to this man when he accepted?

Why would he trust Paul to such a degree? (Remember what you learned from Paul's first journey.)

3. Read Hebrews 12-13 and record new insights.

Fourth Day

1. Read Acts 16:6-40. Why did Paul and his companions choose not to pass through Asia?

What happened as a result of their obedience?

What does their experience teach you?

2. List the major events of Paul's stay at Philippi.

3. Challenge Question: Why didn't Paul visit a synagogue while at Philippi? You may need to call some of your group members for help.

4. Considering everything that had taken place at Philippi, what does Acts 16:25 say to you about Paul and Silas?

Can Jesus make this kind of difference in your life?

If so, how?

What does this incident tell you about the power of intimacy with Christ?

Are you starting to see why intimacy, and not activity, is the key?
Explain.

5. Read James 1-3. James was the Lord's half-brother, born to Joseph and Mary after the

birth of Jesus. He was one of the pillars of the church in Jerusalem. Because you've already studied about Paul and Barnabas's visit to Jerusalem (Acts 15:1-29), and their time with James (Acts 15:13), the book of James should be much more meaningful to you. Record any new insights.

Fifth Day—*Memorize Hebrews 4:9*

1. Read Acts 17 and use the maps to follow Paul's journey. Who opposed Paul in Thessalonica?

Why?

What does the last phrase in Acts 17:6 communicate about the power and authority in the gospel?

How does this power encourage you?

2. How did the people of Berea respond to Paul's message?

How do you think Paul felt when he saw their hunger?

Why did he leave Berea?

3. Where did Paul go after he left Berea?

What did he do there?

Was he persecuted?

What impresses you the most about Paul's stay in Athens?

Do you better understand Acts 9:16?
Explain.

4. Read James 4-5 and record new insights.

Sixth Day

1. Read Acts 18:1-22 and use the maps to follow Paul's journey. Where did Paul go after he left Athens?

With whom did he stay?

What did he do while Silas and Timothy were in Macedonia?

What did Paul do differently after Silas and Timothy arrived at Corinth?

What does this difference teach you?

2. How long did Paul stay in Corinth?

Why did he leave?

Where did he go when he left Corinth?

How was he received?

3. After Paul left Ephesus, where did he go (Acts 18:22)?

How do you think Paul felt as he visited the church at Jerusalem and Antioch?

What would you have shared with them about your journey?

4. What was the most important thing you learned from Paul's second journey?

5. Read this week's lesson and record any new insights.

6. Read Jude. Jude was the brother of James (Jude 1), and the half-brother of Jesus (his name is interpreted Judas in Matthew 13:55 and Mark 6:3). He was one of the leaders in the early church. Record any new insights.

The Life of Paul
(E, 2, 3, and 4)

E. Paul's Life as a Disciple

2. Paul's Trip to Jerusalem (Acts 15:1-29)

As I started writing this section, I spent much time reading Acts 15 through 18. I was almost overwhelmed with the life of Paul, for I saw in a new light the suffering he encountered as he carried the gospel to the world. The ministry the Lord gave him produced abundant fruit, which encouraged me, but the Lord began to reveal some fresh insights about the cost of discipleship. I couldn't help but reflect back to Acts 9:15-16. Oh the truth in those verses! Paul carried the name of the Lord to the Gentiles and kings and the sons of Israel, but he paid a tremendous price in the process. Being a disciple cost him his life. Isn't that exciting?

I kept asking, "How could Paul persevere?" Then, more than ever before I realized that the Lord alone caused him to persevere. God's grace gave him strength to endure his hardship (2Corinthians 12:9). God will provide this same grace as we walk out His calling in our lives. We should be encouraged as we study this section, for we will see for ourselves that God is sufficient and ready to meet every need.

Before Paul embarked on his second missionary journey, he and Barnabas traveled to Jerusalem in response to a disturbance that had taken place in Antioch. Men from Judea had come to Antioch preaching that Gentiles could not be saved without circumcision (v. 1). After much debate, Paul and Barnabas traveled to Jerusalem to meet with the Jerusalem council. Peter was there as well; after Peter, Paul and Barnabas shared what had taken place among the Gentiles. The council agreed that the Gentile believers did not need to be circumcised—that salvation for Jews and Gentiles alike came by grace through faith (verses 9-11). The council chose two men, Judas and Silas, to return to Antioch with Paul and Barnabas.

3. Paul's Return to Antioch (Acts 15:30-35)

Paul, Barnabas, Judas, and Silas returned to Antioch with the council's decision. The people rejoiced when they heard the good news. After Judas and Silas had delivered their message, Judas returned to Jerusalem, but Silas remained. Paul and Barnabas stayed in Antioch teaching and preaching the good news of Jesus Christ.

4. Paul's Second Missionary Journey (Acts 15:36-18:22)

In this section you will observe Paul's travels throughout his second missionary journey. (Please follow along on the maps.)

Paul had problems in Antioch even before he departed (Acts 15:36-41). He suggested to Barnabas that they return to every city they had visited on their first journey (v. 36). Barnabas agreed, but wanted to take along John Mark, who had previously deserted them (vv. 37-38). The dispute caused such disharmony that Barnabas took John Mark and sailed to Cyprus (Barnabas' home [Acts 4:36]), and Paul chose Silas and left for Syria and Cilicia.

Can you imagine how Paul must have felt as he began his second journey? You and I both know the pain of having to disagree with someone you love and respect. Paul and Barnabas had lived together, taught together, suffered together, and been used of the Lord together, but here they parted company for a season over John Mark. Their disagreement did not cause them to terminate their friendship; the Lord of love, who lived in each of them, would ensure that. At the same time, however, Paul must have felt somewhat discouraged as he prepared to leave on his second journey.

Have you ever noticed that Satan tries to discourage us immediately before the Lord is preparing to use us? One thing I always experience before I teach the Word of God, without exception, is spiritual warfare. The one who hates us (Satan) is forever attempting to direct our eyes off of the calling and onto some worldly situation or circumstance. He comes at us in so many, many ways. In this situation, Paul faced one of Satan's frontal assaults, but he laid aside his feelings and traveled through Syria and Cilicia strengthening the churches (v.41). Press on, Paul—you are doing great!

In Acts 16:1-5, Paul and Silas traveled through Derbe and Lystra. Do you remember how Paul was treated at Lystra on his first journey? Can you believe he had the boldness to go back? Paul truly loved these believers, so there was no question in his mind that he needed to return. Paul had no fear of death (Philippians 1:23-24). He had watched

Stephen die peacefully (Acts 7:60), so he was ready and willing to die at any time. Do you view death in this manner? If not, what is keeping you from doing so?

Timothy joined Paul and Silas in Lystra for the remainder of the journey (vv.1-3). Paul discipled Timothy; Timothy's training started here. From all indications, Timothy had seen Paul stoned during his first visit to Lystra (refer to last week's notes). Paul had led him to the Lord, for he refers to Timothy as his child in the faith (1Timothy 1:2). What a wonderful opportunity Timothy had to learn from his teacher, for now he would travel with him and observe his every action. The amazing thing about their friendship is that Timothy trusted Paul enough to allow Paul to circumcise him. Timothy had truly seen Jesus in Paul's life, and instant trust had resulted. He is the same man Paul later addresses in 1Timothy and 2Timothy.

Now read Acts 16:6-10. From Lystra they passed through the Phrygian and Galatian region and came to Troas. They desired to go to Asia and Bithynia, but the Holy Spirit would not allow it. Oh how we must listen to the voice of the Lord. As a result of their obedience, Paul received a vision to go to Macedonia, and the gospel was proclaimed in Europe. (The Lord allowed them to go to Asia later.) Isn't it wonderful that when the Lord says "no!" to one of our requests, He is preparing to say "yes!" to something even better!

You should now read Acts 16:11-40. The following occurred when the disciples reached Philippi:

(1) Lydia and her household believed.

(2) Paul cast a demon out of the slave girl.

(3) The slave girl's masters seized Paul and Silas and had them thrown into prison.

(4) Paul and Silas prayed and sang hymns of praise to God (illustrating that there is true victory in a life committed to intimacy with Christ).

(5) The Lord brought an earthquake; the doors of the prison were opened and everyone's chains were unfastened.

(6) The Philippian jailer accepted Christ (as did his entire household).

(7) Paul and Silas left Philippi.

Observe the fruit of their ministry, but also note the suffering involved along the way.

The Lord truly was using these experiences to build character in Paul's life. Paul's intimacy with Christ, however, allowed him to view these events from God's perspective. Read 2Corinthians 4:16-18 to gain insight into Paul's attitude about suffering.

From Philippi they traveled to Thessalonica (Acts 17:1-9), where several came to know the Lord (v.4). When Paul entered a new city, he almost always taught at the synagogue first—as was the case at Thessalonica (vv.1-2). (This order did not occur in Philippi because no synagogue was there; it was a Roman colony.) He presented the gospel to the Jews first and branched out from there. Paul loved his people (Romans 9:1-5), even though he had been sent to the Gentiles. But Thessalonica's non-believing Jews, as a result of jealousy, started a riot, causing Paul and his companions to travel to Berea. Paul's heart must have been broken when these Jews became jealous over the way the Lord had used him. The true disciple will be careful not to become jealous when the Lord uses others to bring glory to Himself. Only those who share intimacy with Christ can overcome the paralyzing sin of jealously.

At Berea, many received the Word with great eagerness (Acts 17:10-15). I know this reception must have encouraged Paul a great deal, for nothing excites a teacher more than hungry students (1Thessalonians 3:7-9). But when the Jews of Thessalonica heard of these events, they came to Berea and started another riot. (Jealousy can imprison us and destroy our ability to hear from God.) Consequently, Paul traveled to Athens while Silas and Timothy remained at Berea.

Are you starting to see the trend? Paul would preach in a city and people would come to know the lord, but unbelievers would either attack Paul physically or try to contradict his message. Why then should we think it strange when we are persecuted (1Peter 4:12-13)?

Paul's stay in Athens must have been very interesting (Acts 17:16-34) because of the types of people with whom Paul spoke. Along with the Jews and God-fearing Gentiles, he also addressed the Epicurean and Stoic philosophers. The Epicurean philosophers believed that pleasure—not absolute truth—defined existence, while the Stoic philosophers were very moral, but upheld individual independence. Can you imagine addressing these philosophers with the gospel of Jesus Christ, especially in the midst of the Areopagus (v. 22)? Paul's gospel totally contradicted everything for which they stood. Is it any wonder that they sneered when he told them about the resurrection of the dead (v. 32)? Paul left after delivering his sermon, yet some believed (v. 34).

From Athens, Paul traveled to Corinth (Acts 18:1-17). Here he worked with Aquila and Priscilla, but when Silas and Timothy arrived from Macedonia, he devoted himself completely to the Word and to the ministry. (What would happen in Christian circles today if every minister of the gospel desired and had the opportunity to carry on his ministry in this manner?) As usual, Paul first went to the Jews. But when they rejected the gospel, he went to the Gentiles; many of them believed (v. 8). Paul settled in Corinth for more than a year and a half, but left after being persecuted by the Jews.

After leaving Corinth he sailed to Ephesus (Acts 18:18-21). Although he was well received there, he stayed only briefly. In visiting Ephesus Paul visited Asia. God allowed him to do so only after he had obeyed by going to Macedonia first, thereby taking the gospel to Europe. When Paul left Ephesus, he sailed to Caesarea, and then traveled to Jerusalem to greet the church. Next he went to Antioch, where he stayed for some time before embarking on his third missionary journey (Acts 18:22-23).

Paul covered considerable territory on his second journey—2000 miles. They were hard, strenuous miles, filled with trials and difficulties. Do you comprehend how much Paul loved the Lord? Do you see why he could make such statements as those of Philippians 3:7-8 and 1Corinthians 9:16 and 19? Read them and meditate on what they have to say. Paul was sold out to Jesus Christ, and that is what the Lord wants from us. He wants us to live separately from the world and be unreservedly available to Him (Romans 12:1-2). Are you willing to pay the price? Are you willing to become a disciple in the truest sense of the word?

Next week we will follow Paul as he travels on his third missionary journey. Should be fun!

The Life of Paul
(E, 5)

First Day—Memorize Hebrews 4:10

1. Read Acts 18:23-28. Paul starts his third missionary journey. Be sure to use the maps.

What does Acts 18:23 say to you about Paul's desire to make disciples?

2. Read Acts 18:24-28 and write down everything you can about Apollos.

3. What impresses you the most about Apollos?

What did you observe about his life that you would like incorporated into yours?

4. Paul had not yet returned to Ephesus. You will study about Paul's return visit to Ephesus in tomorrow's questions. In the meantime, read Ephesians 1-3. Paul wrote this epistle after spending a large quantity of time in Ephesus. (He spent much time there on his third missionary journey, Acts 19.) He wrote this book during his first imprisonment in Rome. (You will study Paul's voyage to Rome next week.) Record your new insights. Write down any new prayer requests in your prayer journal each day this week. Also, list any answered prayer.

Second Day

1. Read Acts 19. What was "John's baptism" (v. 3)?

What does verse 6 communicate to you?

2. How long was Paul at Ephesus?

What did he do there?

How many people in Asia heard the Word of the Lord through Paul?

3. What do you learn from Acts 19:13-17?

What does this lesson teach you about dealing with matters about which you know little?

4. What significant events occurred in Acts 19:18-20?

5. Read Ephesians 4-6 and record new insights. Paul wrote this epistle after spending much time in Ephesus and during his first imprisonment in Rome.

Third Day—*Memorize Hebrews 4:12*

1. Read Acts 19:21-41. Which of Paul's traveling companions were sent to Macedonia? Remember this!

2. Why was Paul unpopular in Ephesus?

Will we be unpopular for the same reason?

Explain.

When was the last time you were harassed for your faith?

What encouraged you the most as you read about Paul's experience at Ephesus?

3. Read Acts 20:1-12. Where did Paul travel in verses 1-6? Follow his route on the map.

What familiar name is mentioned in verse 4?

4. How long did Paul preach at Troas (vv. 7-12)?

What does this timing say to you about Paul's desire to preach the gospel?

What happened with Eutychus?

How would you have responded to this situation?

5. Read Romans 1-2. Romans is a great book. Paul wrote this epistle on his third missionary journey while at Corinth before having visited Rome. Record your new insights in your notebook.

Fourth Day

1. Read Acts 20:13-38. Use the map to follow Paul's journeys in verses 13-16. Find

Miletus on the map. Who visited Paul there (vv. 17-18)?

Why were these people so special to Paul?

2. What do Paul's statements in Acts 20:19-20 tell you about Paul?

Are you willing to stand on the Word of God in this manner? (Think about your answer and explain your position completely).

3. Read Romans 3-4. Record new insights.

Fifth Day—*Memorize Hebrews 4:16*
1. From Acts 20:21, what did Paul teach?

Define "repentance" and "faith."

Can you obtain salvation without repentance?
Explain.

How do Acts 11:18 and 2Timothy 2:25 tie in with this topic?

2. What did you learn about Paul in Acts 20:22-25?

Why would he view death in the manner described here?

How do you view death?

What does Acts 20:24 tell you about Paul's determination to complete the ministry the Lord had given him?

Pray that more people in the body of Christ will develop this attitude. Pray that you can have this attitude.

3. What kind of statement does Acts 20:26-27 make about Paul?

Could you say the same about yourself?

If not, what are you doing to change the situation?

4. What did Paul instruct the elders to do in verses 28-32?

Are you strong enough in the Word to detect false teachers when you hear them?
Is this course helping you in this area?
If so, how?

5. Read Romans 5-7 and record new insights.

Sixth Day

1. What does Acts 20:33-35 say about Paul's lifestyle?

Do you think these habits helped or hindered the effectiveness of Paul's ministry? Why?

2. Do those around you view you as a hard worker?

How does 2Thessalonians 3:6-12 relate?

God gets much glory when we do our work as unto Him. Don't expect to be an effective witness if you behave in a slothful and lethargic (lazy) manner.

3. After reading Acts 20:36-38, would you say that Paul had the love, support, and respect of these believers?

What touches you most about the statements in these verses?

Would you like to be loved in this manner?

What must occur in our lives before this type of love can become part of our experience?

4. Read Acts 21:1-14. Follow Paul's route as he traveled back to Caesarea (use the maps).

What encouraged you as you read these verses?

What did you learn from verse 13?

Are you starting to see how single-minded Paul was when it came to serving Jesus?

What will it take for you to develop a similar attitude?

5. Read this week's lesson and record any new insights.

6. Read Romans 8-9; Record new insights in your notebook.

The Life of Paul
(E, 5)

E. Paul's Life as a Disciple

5. Paul's Third Missionary Journey (Acts 18:23-21:14)

Are you ready to learn about "follow up"? You cannot read Acts 18:23-21:14 without sensing Paul's love for those to whom he had ministered on his first and second journeys. After he came to Antioch (Acts 18:22), Paul spent some time there and departed again for Galatia and Phrygia (v. 23). The last phrase of verse 23 states that Paul strengthened all the disciples in these areas. In other words, he returned to take them deeper in their walk with Christ. He knew their only hope was to know their Savior as their "life." If you read Ephesians 1:15-23 and 3:14-19, you will understand Paul's goal for every disciple.

Acts 18:24-28 introduces Apollos, an eloquent learned man who was mighty in the Scriptures. He taught accurately about Jesus in Ephesus, but was acquainted only with the baptism of John. And what was the baptism of John? We find our answer in Acts 19:4, which says, *"John baptized with the baptism of repentance, telling the people to believe in Him who was coming after him, that is, in Jesus."* John's baptism dealt with repentance. (Repentance means more than just feeling sorry for your sin; it means choosing to do something about it. Read Luke 3:3 and 3:8.) John knew that true repentance brought a change of lifestyle (fruit), which confirmed a change of heart. After repenting, the people were to believe in the One who would come after him—none other than Jesus Christ. Evidently Apollos had heard of the baptism of John through those who had seen John baptizing at Bethany beyond Jordan (John 1:28).

When Priscilla and Aquila heard Apollos, "they took him aside and explained to him the way of God more accurately" (v. 26). Put simply, they discipled Apollos. Afterwards, he traveled to Achaia and was used mightily of the Lord at Corinth. But his departure meant that the people of Ephesus lost the benefit of continuing in his teaching. However, Priscilla and Aquila had fulfilled 2Timothy 2:2 in Apollos' life, and that was all that mattered. God had prepared an even greater teacher to return to Ephesus, a teacher who would turn the whole city into an uproar. The stage was most definitely set for Paul's return to Ephesus.

Acts 19:1-7 is somewhat controversial and must be handled carefully. One doctrine that has come from these verses states that the laying on of hands is the only means by which a person can receive the Holy Spirit. This idea cannot be true because in Acts 10:44-48 the Gentiles received the Holy Spirit as they listened to Peter's message. No hands were laid on these Gentiles, but they received the Spirit the same way the apostles had in Acts 2 (Acts 11:15). We could add much more here, but for the sake of time and space we must proceed.

Another doctrine states that only those who speak in tongues have received the Baptism by the Holy Spirit. Many different ideas exist concerning this issue, but think about this one for a moment. Paul teaches that "all" believers are baptized into the body of Christ through the avenue of the Holy Spirit—at the point of salvation (1Corinthians 12:13). Now look at 1Corinthians 12:30. Not everyone who was baptized into the body of Christ spoke in tongues! Therefore, we cannot assume that speaking in tongues is necessary to confirm that a person has been baptized by the Holy Spirit

We must never interpret Scripture based on our experience. We must make certain that our experience lines up with the principles taught in the Word of God. 1Corinthians 13 is our ultimate goal.

The following statements have helped me tremendously in dealing with these issues:

(1) Baptism by the Spirit is initiatory and occurs when we repent of our sins and submit our lives to Jesus Christ. In contrast, we need to be filled with the Spirit over and over as we walk with Christ (Ephesians 5:18).

(2) None of the apostolic sermons or epistles charges believers to be baptized by the Spirit (for it happened at the point of salvation), but they do exhort the believer to be filled with that same Spirit.

After Paul ministered to the twelve in Acts 19:1-7, he entered the synagogue and reasoned with the people about the kingdom of God (v. 8). He taught here for three months and evidently had a very successful ministry. However, when opposition arose he took his students to the school of Tyrannus and taught there for two years (vv. 9-10). But look at verse 10—*"All who lived in Asia heard the Word of the Lord, both Jews and*

Greeks." Isn't the sovereignty of God amazing? Paul had desired to visit Asia during the beginning stages of his second journey (Acts 16:6). However, God, Who had a better idea, did not grant Paul's desire. He waited until now to use Paul to spread the gospel throughout Asia.

The lesson here is that God's ways are always better than our ways. Is God telling you to put off doing something until later? If so, He just happens to have a plan that is greater than anything you could imagine (Ephesians 3:20).

In Acts 19:11-20 the Lord performed extraordinary miracles through Paul. It also tells about the seven sons of Sceva. The bottom line here is that the world cannot imitate or counterfeit the ministry of Christ. It will not work! Even when the world tries, the Lord still brings glory to Himself (verses 16-17). Do you see how God uses all situations to bring the lost out of darkness and into His marvelous light (Philippians 1:12-18)? Also notice that many who had practiced magic brought their books and burned them (vv.18-20), which was nothing short of a miracle!

Paul sent Timothy and Erastus to Macedonia to prepare the people for his coming (Acts 19:21-22). These verses confirm that Timothy traveled with Paul. Paul stayed in Ephesus, but the Lord's work through him caused quite a disturbance (Acts 19:23-41). Verses 26-27 are the key passages in this section. Paul's persecution resulted from his proving that the "gods made with hands are no gods at all." What a wonderful thing for God to do through Paul! He can do the same through us if we will but write His Word on our hearts.

Paul left Ephesus and passed through Macedonia, exhorting the brethren (Acts 20:1-2). He then came to Greece, where he spent three months, but left after the Jews plotted against his life. Acts 20:3-6 tells that he returned through Macedonia and sailed from Philippi of Macedonia to Troas. (Find Macedonia on the map and locate the cities he would have visited there.)

Paul's stay in Troas was fascinating (Acts 20:7-12). Would you have enjoyed listening to such a lengthy sermon? Can you imagine the hunger in these believers' hearts? Of course those who can't stay awake are always present. In this case Eutychus dozed off and fell out of a third-story window. (It was not just a catnap, but a "deep sleep." Hope he didn't snore!) He was picked up dead (v.9), but Paul embraced him and his life was restored (v.10-12). Then Paul did something that boggles the mind. He went back and continued to preach until daybreak! What boldness!

Acts 20:13-16 details Paul's journey to Miletus. I believe his message to the elders in Ephesus is one of the most moving sections of Acts (Acts 20:17-35). Paul has much to say about discipleship in these passages.

Verse 19: Paul spoke of how he served the Lord humbly and with tears in the midst of his trials. The Lord used Paul in a powerful way at Ephesus, but he suffered greatly in the process. God gives grace to the humble, but resists the proud (James 4:6).

Verse 20: When teaching the church at Ephesus, Paul held back nothing that was profitable. If our hearts are right, we will avoid teaching what tickles the ear and instead teach what is beneficial. Paul also taught publicly and from house to house. He taught not only in large groups but also in smaller groups. A disciple soon learns that the most profitable work is done in a small group setting.

Verse 21: Paul not only taught faith, but also repentance. Repentance means to do something about your sin, to turn from it and to desire to walk in a holy manner. Repentance is neglected in many "religious" circles of our day. The disciple must be careful that he or she teaches the whole council of God.

Verses 22-25: Here we see Paul's attitude toward suffering and death. He seemed to have no fear of either. We also see his motivation to "finish his course." Paul longed to complete the ministry the Lord had given him, *"to testify solemnly of the gospel of the grace of God,"* and he wanted to do so in Jerusalem! A disciple senses a calling to testify of this gospel in the area of his gifting (1Peter 4: 10). Nothing, absolutely nothing, should hinder the disciple from doing so.

Verses 26-27: Paul was innocent of the blood of all men because he had taught the whole purpose of God. He had taught the Word of God without compromise. He knew he could die without concern that his listeners had heard only partial truth.

Verses 28-31: Paul knew that false teachers would arise after his departure, so he warned the elders to be on guard for the flock. A disciple loves those he has taught and is very much concerned about their welfare after he is gone.

Verse 32: Paul commended the elders to God and to the word of His grace. Paul knew the Word was the only thing that could build them up. A disciple constantly reminds those he has taught about the importance of the Word.

Verse 33-35: Paul worked for his income. He not only used it for his own personal needs, but also for the needs of his companions. For Paul, giving was truly more blessed than receiving. A disciple will learn this lesson as he shares his life and material possessions with those he has grown to love and appreciate.

Verse 36-38: These verses describe the people's reaction to Paul's departure. I cannot imagine what was going through Paul's mind at this time. Can you sense how much they loved him? This love is the payment that a disciple receives as he lays down his life for his friends. Receiving the love from those he has discipled, and witnessing their growth in the Lord, makes the disciple's life the most fulfilling life imaginable (1Thessalonians 2:19, 20; 3:8).

Acts 21:1-14 wraps up this section. Paul traveled from Miletus to Tyre. There his disciples told him (through the Spirit) not to set foot in Jerusalem (v. 4). From Tyre Paul traveled through Ptolemais and then to Caesarea. Here he was told again—by Agabus, through the Spirit—that he would suffer in Jerusalem (v. 11). But Paul responded by saying, "For I am ready not only to be bound, but even to die at Jerusalem for the name of the Lord Jesus" (v. 13). I don't view this as an act of disobedience. I see Paul, rather, as having no fear of suffering, even when it most certainly awaited him. He had endured a great deal in his walk with the Lord, but the Lord had always come through. Why would He choose not to do so now?

Are you starting to see the degree to which Paul loved those into whom he had poured his life? 1Corinthians 13 was fulfilled through Paul on a regular basis. And the same can happen to us! Isn't that exciting! Isn't that challenging! What could be more fulfilling than knowing, really knowing, Christ, and having Him minister to the needs of others through us?

Next week we will cover Paul's time in Jerusalem and his trip to Rome. Don't miss it. What we learn will be very encouraging.

The Life of Paul
(E, 6, 7, and 8)
(F, 1, 2, 3, and 4)

First Day—*Memorize Ephesians 4:32*

1. Read Acts 21:15-23:30. What impressed you the most about Paul in these Scriptures?

What keeps you from making the same statement about yourself that Paul made about himself in Acts 23:1?

2. Since this week's lesson is longer than usual, go ahead and read the portion titled *Paul's Time In Jerusalem.* Record any new insights.

3. Read Romans 10-12 and record new insights. Write down any new prayer requests in your prayer journal, each day this week. Also record all answered prayer.

Second Day

1. Read Acts 23:31-26:32. Follow Paul's travels on the map. What does Acts 24:16 tell you about Paul's heart?

In Acts 26:13-19 Paul refers to his vision. Why did Jesus appear to him (v.16)?

What was Paul's mission?

2. Read Acts 26:20 again. What does the phrase "that they should repent and turn to God, performing deeds appropriate to repentance" communicate to you?

According to Acts 26:22, from where did Paul's sermon material come?

When you share about Christ, from where does your material come?

3. Go ahead and read the portion of this week's lesson titled *Paul's Time In Caesarea.* Record any new insights.

4. Read Romans 13-16 and record new insights in your notebook.

Third Day—*Memorize Colossians 2:13*
1. Read Acts 27:1-28:31. Take advantage of the map titled ***Paul's Voyage to Rome.***
What was the most important thing you learned about Paul as he traveled from Caesarea to Rome?

Once Paul reached Rome, where was he allowed to live?

Did he have a ministry in Rome?

If so, to whom did he minister?

Explain how Romans 8:28 applies to what is mentioned in Acts 28:30-31.

2. We will now begin dealing with Section III, Part F, *How Paul Discipled Timothy*. From our previous lessons, what attracted Timothy to Paul?

How did Paul teach (disciple) Timothy?

3. Read 1Timothy 1. Paul wrote this epistle to Timothy between his first and second imprisonments in Rome. He had placed Timothy in charge of the church at Ephesus (1Timothy 1:3). What impressed you the most about the way Paul communicated with Timothy?

What does verse 5 say to you?

What does verse 19 say to you?

Why must the disciple have a clear conscience?

Write down any new insights.

4. Read 1Timothy 2-3. What did you learn about discipleship from these two chapters?

Write down your new insights.

Fourth Day

1. Read 1Timothy 4. Write down every point of instruction that Paul gave Timothy in verses 12-16.

Has studying this chapter touched you in any way?
If so, how?

Record new insights.

2. Read 1Timothy 5-6. In 1Timothy 6:11-14, how did Paul instruct Timothy concerning his daily walk?

How would you have reacted had Paul written these instructions to you?

Didn't the Lord write these instructions to us through Paul?
Do you see my point?

Record new insights.

Fifth Day—*Memorize 1Thessalonians 5:23*

1. Read 2Timothy 1. Paul wrote this epistle during his second imprisonment in Rome, and shortly before his death. What is the most important thing you learned from this chapter?

Take verses 6-8, 12-14, and 15 and write out what they say to you about your own walk with Christ.

What do they say about the cost of discipleship?

Record any new insights.

2. Read 2Timothy 2. What did you learn about discipleship from verses 1-7?

What does verse 15 say to you?

Please take your time and meditate on these verses before writing down your answers. The information here will help us to become the disciples we need to be.

Record new insights.

Sixth Day

1. Read 2Timothy 3. What does verse 14 teach you about the importance of discipleship?

Why could Paul speak this way?

Do you desire to speak in this manner?

What will it take for you to do so?

Record new insights.

2. Read 2Timothy 4. What do verses 1-8 tell you about Paul and his concern for Timothy?

What do they tell you about Paul's commitment to the truth in God's Word?

Record new insights.

3. Of the things we have studied thus far in the course, what has touched you the most?

4. Make sure that you have read this week's entire lesson.

Record any new insights in your notebook.

The Life of Paul
(E, 6, 7, and 8)
(F, 1, 2, 3, and 4)

E. Paul's Life as a Disciple

This week's lesson is longer than usual. We will make up for it next week with a shorter lesson. As we cover Parts 6-8 of Section E, we will only hit the highlights. This plan does not mean that this segment of Paul's life is less significant than the others, but we will condense it for the sake of time and space. Hold on as we watch the Lord take Paul through Jerusalem, on to Caesarea, and then to Rome.

6. Paul's Time in Jerusalem (Acts 21:15-23:30)

According to Acts 21:17-20, Paul had an opportunity to share with the leaders of the church at Jerusalem. As is confirmed in verse 20, Paul's words brought much joy to his listeners. Acts 21:21 tells that Paul's teaching had been twisted by those who opposed his ministry. Every disciple will encounter this problem. As we teach the full counsel of God's Word, some will always try to distort our message. For this reason we must pay close attention to what we teach (1Timothy 4:16) and handle accurately the Word of Truth (2Timothy 2:15). The remainder of this chapter, Acts 21:22-40, tells that Paul's enemies (the Jews) tried to kill him, but his arrest by the Roman soldiers—through God's sovereignty—saved him from death.

The Romans allowed Paul to address his enemies as he was taken into custody. In Acts 22:1-21 he shared his testimony as to how he met Christ. When I read these verses I am amazed at Paul's boldness. His message contained absolutely no compromise. The authority with which he spoke must have been something to behold.

Acts 22:22-23 records the mob's reaction to Paul's message. The Jews were so enraged that Paul had to be rushed into the Roman barracks (v. 24). Acts 22:24-29 records what occurred once he arrived at the barracks.

Does it still surprise you when people respond negatively to your message of Jesus Christ? When this type of response occurs, does it bring you to such a point of despair that you lose your boldness and joy? Paul's boldness did not diminish in the least as a result of these events. Acts 22:30-23:30 records that Paul spoke out boldly before the Council (Sanhedrin) soon after—so boldly in fact that more than 40 of the Jews swore to neither eat nor drink until they had killed him (23:12-13). When the Roman commander learned of their plot, Paul was taken to appear before Felix.

Can you believe what Paul endured for the cause of the gospel? His life reminds me that I don't yet know the true meaning of suffering. Isn't it exciting to realize that we serve a God who can supply such abundant grace!

7. Paul's Time in Caesarea (Acts 23:31-26:32)

The Scriptures that relate to this section are Acts 23:31-26:32. At Caesarea, Paul appeared before Felix (Acts 24), Festus (Acts 25), and King Agrippa (Acts 26). He displayed the same boldness with which he had spoken earlier as he addressed each of these three men (along with the audiences present). His message especially touched Felix and King Agrippa (Acts 24:25, Acts 26:28), but Festus thought Paul was out of his mind (Acts 26:24). This account illustrates that the lost will react to the disciple in a variety of ways. We must never be shaken, regardless of the response.

Several passages here reveal a great deal about the condition of Paul's heart. First, in Acts 24:16 Paul walked with a clear conscience. A clear conscience is a necessity if the message is to have authority. Paul was not disobedient to the vision and calling on his life (Acts 26:13, 19). The Lord appointed Paul as a minister and witness of the things he had seen and would see. He was to share what he had learned with Jews and Gentiles alike. He was also called to preach repentance—true repentance, which brought a change of behavior (Acts 26:20). And finally, Acts 26:22 relates the key to the authority in Paul's message. When he preached, he preached directly from God's Word. He didn't have to use magazine articles, the editorial section of a newspaper, or even quotes from the previous night's newscast. His words came solely from Scripture. Is it any wonder that Paul's messages were so powerful, yet so controversial?

As a result of Paul's appeal (Acts 25:11), Festus sent him to Rome.

8. Paul's Trip to Rome (Acts 27:1-28:31)

Acts 27 and 28 detail this segment of Paul's life. He faced more trials, for the trip was very trying and very "stormy." At times Paul and his traveling companions must have lost all hope of remaining alive (Acts 27:20). But the God Who had protected Paul in the past would protect him in this situation as well. He sent His angel to reveal to Paul that no lives would be lost (Acts 27:22-25). God had also promised Paul (as far back as Acts 23:11) that he would visit Rome. Therefore, when his companions lost hope, Paul's faith brought encouragement.

Not only did the Lord protect Paul while at sea, but He also continued to do so upon his arrival in Rome. Paul lived in his own rented quarters and openly taught many about Jesus Christ (Acts 28:30-31). Isn't it amazing how God can use the most trying circumstances for our good? Why is it that we worry and fret when faced with uncertainties? If we will but use our faith, God will do for us what He did for Paul. And what did He do for Paul?

He confirmed that all things most definitely work for good to those who love God and are called according to His purpose (Romans 8:28)! Thank you, Jesus!!

F. How Paul Discipled Timothy

I am convinced that this section is one of the most important of the course. Many of us are asking, "What do I do now that I am learning to sit with Christ? Just how do I go about discipling someone in the faith?" These questions are big, but they can be answered by merely considering Paul and Timothy's relationship. Let's examine how Paul discipled Timothy.

1. What Attracted Timothy to Paul

If you review your notes from Paul's first and second missionary journeys, you will find that Timothy watched as Paul was stoned at Lystra (Acts 14:19, 2 Timothy 3:10-11). Few would have returned to Lystra after experiencing such trials, but Paul returned with boldness (Acts 14:21·22). Timothy saw a power and authority within him that was nothing short of supernatural. Paul's love for the Lord and for His people must have been an intriguing sight for the young Timothy. This love had to be what attracted Timothy to this man of God.

As we mature in the faith, others will be attracted to Christ's life within us. When the

Lord allows trials to cross our paths, the world is bound to see His power manifested in a way that is both intriguing and captivating. Then opportunities arise for Christ to teach through us what we have learned while sitting alone in His presence.

We don't do anything "for" God, but God does all things through us. One of the requirements of becoming a disciple is to understand that we are powerless to change lives—even our own. Only God is in the transformation business (2 Corinthians 3:18). Therefore, I am not required to run about frantically trying to find someone into whom to pour my life. If we are falling more deeply in love with Christ on a moment-by-moment basis, God will ensure that we meet the right people at the right time. God allowed Timothy to live in Lystra. But Timothy did not encounter Paul until Paul was mature enough to disciple him. God is sovereign, and He is just waiting for us to come to Him wholeheartedly, to know Him—really know Him so He might open doors of ministry that will astound us.

2. How Paul Taught Timothy

One might think that Paul used some secret formula to disciple Timothy. After all, is it unreasonable to imagine that a man of Paul's caliber had a special corner on discipleship? I believe it would be!

Here's the key: Paul loved Timothy and wanted to spend time with him. These characteristics, along with a few other factors, made discipleship as natural a process as breathing.

First, Paul was grounded in God's Word. He was more mature than Timothy and stayed ahead of him in his spiritual growth. The disciple must continually progress in his walk with Christ, for he can never take anyone further than he is himself. Please don't let this statement intimidate you. Satan spends much of his time trying to convince believers that they don't measure up. I know that this fact is true, for I have met hoards of believers who tremble at the mere mention of the word "discipleship." Please hear me: You don't need a doctorate in theology to pour your life into others. I think it is time we realized our capabilities and acted accordingly. Are you willing to step out on God's promises and fulfill your commission (Matthew 28:19-20, Philippians 4:13)? If so, we will see revival take place in this country, and—even more important—in our own homes, churches, and hearts.

Second, Paul desired to disciple Timothy. This desire is confirmed in Acts 16:3, which says that "Paul wanted this man to go with him." Do you find yourself desiring to pour your life into others? If not, you need to ask yourself why you are lacking in this area. We cannot walk in intimacy with the King of Kings and not long to see others reach their full potential in Christ.

Third, Timothy wanted to spend time with Paul. An amazing thing happened in Acts 16:3. Paul circumcised Timothy as soon as they began traveling together. Timothy surely would have balked at this idea had he possessed misgivings about their relationship. This event confirms that Timothy was sold out to the idea of spending time with his teacher. The people into whom we pour our lives must be faithful to their commitment to Christ, as well as their commitment to us. Paul realized this truth and later told Timothy to pour his life into faithful men (2Timothy 2:2).

Fourth, Paul loved Timothy, even to the point that he viewed him as his son in the faith (1Timothy 1:2, 18; 2Timothy 1:2-4). As a result of this love, Timothy must have viewed Paul as his spiritual father. The man who discipled me loved me so much that it impacted me for life. I will never be the same as a result of the time we spent together. I would have done anything (within reason) for him, and I feel the same way some 18 years later. The words of Jesus were fulfilled as we matured together (John 13:34-35).

Fifth, Paul and Timothy spent large quantities of time together. Time together is an important but demanding ingredient. Discipleship cannot occur unless we consciously set aside time for those we want to encourage. We must remember this principal as we live in our busy society. As we begin meeting with those to whom we are drawn, we should set realistic goals. An hour a week is a good starting point. The relationship will build from there as we allow the Spirit of God to do His work.

Sixth, Paul, a man, discipled Timothy, a man. Men should disciple men and women should disciple women. I have found that this method is the most effective, unless of course you are discipling a person of the opposite sex in your immediate family. Even in such cases, it is still more effective if men are with men and women are with women. Men tend to express themselves more openly with other men; the same is true for women. If you are having difficulty understanding my reasoning here, just wait. You will agree with these statements as you become more involved with discipleship and small-group situations.

To sum up the six main ingredients that served as the glue in Paul and Timothy's relationship: (1) Paul stayed ahead of Timothy in his spiritual growth; (2) Paul wanted to disciple Timothy; (3) Timothy wanted Paul to disciple him, and Timothy was a faithful man; (4) Paul loved Timothy and vice versa; (5) Paul spent large quantities of time with Timothy; (6) Timothy was the same gender as Paul.

See, this discipleship thing is not so difficult after all. I can't wait to see what the Lord has in store for you as these truths become more and more a part of your life.

3. What Paul Taught Timothy

We could spend days here, for the wealth of information and insight that Paul passed to Timothy must have been nothing short of mind-boggling (2Timothy 1:13-14). To understand the scope of what we are dealing with here, you should at some point read Romans through Philemon. Paul authored these epistles, so they should give you a good idea of what Timothy learned from his father in the faith.

Timothy was with Paul (off and on) from the time of Paul's second missionary journey (Acts 16:1-3) until Paul's death (2 Timothy 4:5-7). A few of the doctrines that Timothy would have learned from Paul are:

(1) We have all sinned (Romans 3:23).

(2) The wages of sin is death (Romans 6:23).

(3) Repentance is necessary for salvation. Repentance means to turn from your sinful way (not simply to be sorry for your sin). This repentance brings a new attitude about sin; sin becomes repulsive. This repentance must accompany faith in Christ for salvation to occur. The following verses confirm how Paul viewed repentance (Acts 17:30, 20:21, 26:20, and 2Timothy 2:25).

(4) A believer is declared "not guilty!" in the eyes of God based on faith (Romans 5:1). This doctrine is justification by faith. This faith must be accompanied by repentance.

(5) We have been saved by grace through faith (Ephesians 2:8-9).

(6) No one can work his way into a right standing with God (Romans 3:20), for the Law was given to expose our sin and show us our need for Christ (Galatians 3:24).

(7) We are not under Law, but under grace (Romans 6:14).

(8) The Holy Spirit comes to live in us at the point of salvation (Romans 8:15-16).

(9) Jesus comes to live in us at the point of salvation (Galatians 2:20, Colossians 1:27).

(10) The instant we give our lives to Christ, God says these truths about us (and much, much more):

(a) You are justified and glorified (Romans 8:30).

(b) You are a New Creation (2Corinthians 5:17).

(c) You are the righteousness of God (2Corinthians 5:21).

(d) You are holy and blameless (Ephesians 1:4).

(e) You are accepted (Ephesians 1:6 KJV).

(f) You are seated in the heavenlies with the Father and the Son (Ephesians 2:6).

(g) You are forgiven (Ephesians 4:32, Colossians 2:13).

(h) You are a member of His body (Ephesians 5:30).

(i) You are complete (Colossians 2:10).

This listing of what God says about us as a result of being a member of His family is only partial.

Paul also told Timothy to pay close attention to what he taught (1Timothy 4:16), a lesson that every disciple must learn. He also encouraged Timothy to teach faithful men what he had taught him (2Timothy 2:2) and to continue in the many things he had learned from Paul (2Timothy 3:14). Timothy not only learned truth, but had become convinced of the truth as well (2Timothy 3:14). We too, must become convinced that God's truth is absolute truth before we can speak it with any degree of authority. Paul's view of the Scriptures is given in 2Timothy 3:15-17, the only view that brings depth to the message, power to the ministry, and any lasting fruit. Timothy adopted this view, and thus God used him mightily after Paul's death.

4. Paul's Instruction to A Mature Timothy

We only need one verse of Scripture to determine how much responsibility Paul gave Timothy when he had matured in the faith. 1Timothy 1:3 states, *"As I urged you upon my departure from Macedonia, remain on at Ephesus, in order that you may instruct certain men not to teach strange doctrines."* The book of Acts details how Paul taught longer at Ephesus than at any other location (Acts 20:31). If you had poured your life into the church at Ephesus, and led them into the deeper things of God (Acts 20:17-21, 25-31), you would take comfort in knowing that a man of Timothy's caliber would lead them after the Lord had called you home. If you want to read some "deep" Scripture, read all six chapters of Ephesians (not now, but sometime soon). The church at Ephesus was a very mature church; otherwise it could not have comprehended Paul's message. I personally believe that Timothy was the most seasoned man that Paul could place over these believers. Thus Timothy went to Ephesus.

Can you imagine how it comforted Paul to know that Timothy would continue the work at Ephesus? Paul lived to see the fruit produced from his time with Timothy. Could this same thing happen to you? I believe it can! Would you take the challenge of Romans 12:1 and lose your life to find it (Matthew 10:39)? Would you ask God to give you grace enough to fulfill the great commission (Matthew 28:19-20), so that "as you go" you might make disciples of all peoples?

Learning to Share Your Testimony
(A)

First Day—*Memorize Romans 10:17*

1. Read Acts 22:1-21 and write down the main points that Paul shared in his testimony.

Who was he addressing here?

2. Had you been Paul, what would you have been tempted to add or subtract from this testimony? He was speaking to people who had known him or known about him for many years.

3. Read Matthew 1-3. Matthew, the tax collector and apostle, wrote this gospel. As you read, notice how Jesus loved and discipled the twelve. Record any new insights.

Write down any new prayer requests in your prayer journal each day this week. Also list any answered prayer.

Second Day

1. Read Acts 26: 1-18. Write down the main points that Paul shared in his testimony.

Whom was he addressing here?

2. What similarities are between Paul's testimony in Acts 22 and his testimony in Acts 26?

What differences?

3. Read Matthew 4-5. Record your new insights in your notebook.

Third Day

1. Reflect back on Acts 22 and 26 and try to remember what Paul shared about his B.C. (before Christ) days. Do you think he went into too much or too little detail about that segment of his life?

Why?

2. If you were asked to share about your B.C. days, what would you say about them?

I realize, of course, that if you were saved at a very young age that you won't have much to share about this segment of your life. Wonderful! I only wish that were my case. You can spend more time addressing how you came to Christ and what He has done in your life since.

3. Read Matthew 6-7. Record any new insights.

Fourth Day—*Memorize Acts 4:12*

1. Reflect on Acts 22 and 26 and try to remember what Paul shared about his conversion experience. Did he communicate his testimony by using ten-dollar words or simple, everyday language?

Explain why you think he spoke in this manner.

2. What does the answer to the previous question tell you about how you should share your testimony?

3. Read Matthew 8-9. Record any new insights.

Fifth Day

1. From Acts 22 and 26, along with Philippians 3:4-16, what does Paul say about his life since coming to know Christ?

2. When you share your testimony, what do you say about the changes that have occurred in your life since coming to know Christ?

3. Read Matthew 10:11 and record new insights.

Sixth Day

1. Three basic things should be in our testimony. (1) Our B.C. (before Christ) days. (2) Our salvation experience. (3) What has happened in our lives since coming to know Christ? In your opinion, which one of these categories should be emphasized the most? Why?

Which one should be emphasized the least?
Why?

2. Read this week's lesson and record new insights.

3. Read Matthew 12-13 and record new insights.

Learning to Share Your Testimony
(A)

A. Paul's Testimony

Soon after my salvation experience, I had the wonderful privilege of being discipled by a man who loved me unconditionally, as a disciple must (John 13:34-35). He also displayed (through his lifestyle) the impact God's Word can have on a believer. Read Psalm 119:9-11. I observed a power and authority in him that was nothing short of supernatural. Our time together so touched my life that I wanted everyone I knew to realize the importance of discipleship (my motivation in writing this study). I was discipled, but the man who discipled me had the maturity to lead me straight to Jesus and not to himself. He was mature enough to know that Christ alone can sustain a believer.

Our relationship grew until we began to trust one another to a much greater degree. We did many things that deepened our friendship—even activities besides prayer and Bible study. We ran, played golf, shot basketball—all sorts of fun things.

God's desire was that I might know Christ as my life. God's desire for my friend was the same, but it was also time for 2Timothy 2:2 to be fulfilled to a greater degree within his experience. A disciple will soon learn that truth from God's Word impacts those who have fertile hearts. So the Lord was doing a great work in both of us, even though I was not mature enough to realize it. I thought our relationship was a one-way street, and I even carried guilt because I was taking so much of my friend's "valuable" time. But the Lord gradually showed me that He was teaching both of us as we walked together.

I will never forget the first verse my friend gave me to memorize: Romans 10:17. He gave me a week to memorize it, so I thought it would be a snap. When I tried to recite my verse the next week, however, all I could remember were the first two words. I had forgotten the rest. I felt badly about it, but he encouraged me, and by the end of the following week I had recited it perfectly. I was so excited! I had written the first verse of Scripture on my heart (mind), and I felt as if I could conquer the world! I soon learned, however, that I needed much more than one verse; I learned that I needed all of the verses I could get! This knowledge started a chain reaction that transformed my life, for I had gotten a good taste of the Word of God—a taste which created a hunger in my heart that will never vanish.

Soon after I recited my first verse, my friend asked me to put my story (or testimony of how I found Christ) either on paper or on a cassette tape. I had never done anything like that, so I bought a tape and went to work. I was pleased with the finished product (even to the point of being prideful about it), but when my friend heard its content, he wasn't pleased at all! In fact, he suggested that I do the whole thing over! But what touched me was the manner in which he corrected me. He was correcting me for my good. Consequently, I was willing to listen to his counsel and try again.

I re-recorded the tape, this time including some new material. I added things that I thought would impress him, such as more verses of Scripture. The tape turned out to be much longer, so I knew it would meet his approval. Instead, soon after he heard it, he called me and told me words that ring in my ears to this day. Speaking in love, he said, "When you give your testimony, you don't preach. You always have to remember KISS-Keep It Simple, Stupid. If you have time, read what Paul said about his own salvation experience and get back with me." Only after I had studied Paul's testimony did I come to grips with my own. (Acts 22:1-21 and Acts 26:1-23.) Here are a few things I saw as I studied Acts 22 and 26:

1. Paul spoke of his early life (Acts 22:3, Acts 26:4-5). He spoke of the time he persecuted the church, but did not go into unnecessary detail (Acts 22:4-5, Acts 26:9-11). I am sure he could have told hours of spellbinding stories. He resisted that temptation, however, and got to the "meat" of his testimony—how he met Christ and what had happened in his life since. It is tempting to go into too much detail about our past life of sin. We are almost led to believe that if our testimony is not "bad" enough, no one will listen. Always remember that Jesus has the most powerful testimony known to man, and it does not include one act of sin. Lives are not changed by the listener knowing how "evil" we were, but rather by understanding how we met Jesus and what He is doing in us today. People should know where we have come from, but they need not know every detail. If you found Christ at a young age and have little to share about your B.C. (before Christ) days, "rejoice and be glad." I only wish that were the case with me!!

2. Paul used very simple terms when he spoke of his salvation experience. This simplicity allowed everyone to understand how he had come to Christ (Acts 22:6-16,

Acts 26:12-18). Therefore, if anyone desired to accept Christ, they knew exactly how. Paul was a mature believer in Acts 22 and Acts 26, so he understood the importance of making everything as clear-cut as possible. Had we heard him share his testimony as a new believer, I am sure we would have found it very different from what we read in Acts 22 and 26. But Paul had matured, and the results of that maturity are evident as he shares his testimony while under arrest.

The way I share my testimony has changed somewhat through the years. Now I seem to share less about my past life, and more about Him—how I met Him and what He is doing in my life today. I also find myself simplifying my testimony the more I give it. We should do this as much as possible, eliminating anything that might confuse the listener. We must always remember that we are addressing people who are at varying levels of spiritual maturity. Many will not yet know Christ, so we must learn to relate to them as well as to believers. The goal is to share our testimony in such a way that everyone knows exactly what we are trying to communicate.

3. Paul shared much about what had transpired since his encounter with Christ (Acts 22:17-21, Acts 26:19-23). Also read Philippians 3:4-16. We should too, for this area is one of the listener's main points of interest. Always beware of the person who has much to say about his or her B.C. (before Christ) days and salvation experience, but little to say about Christ's work in him today. If Christ is not deepening our message, we should be quiet and sit for a season. Whenever someone is kind enough to listen, we owe it to him to share a fresh and crisp message. Don't misunderstand me. I will be sharing my salvation experience for the rest of my days. I must, however, walk with Christ in a way that allows Him to mature me. If I do, He will provide a constant stream of new insights that I can share with others.

Three basic steps in presenting our testimony:

1. We should feel free to speak of our B.C. days, but we should be very careful to monitor the depth in which we share them. We don't want Satan to receive any glory from the things of which we are now ashamed (Romans 6:21).

2. We should share how we came to Christ, expressing it in terms that even a child could understand. When we finish sharing our salvation experience, everyone listening should know exactly how to accept Christ.

3. We should say more about what Christ has done in us since we became believers than about our B.C. days. More detail is okay here, but we must always remember to Keep It Simple. To communicate the fact that effective Christian service results from letting Christ work through us, rather than us working "for" Christ, is of utmost importance.

Learning to Share Your Testimony
(B)

B. Application Weeks (Sharing Your Testimony), *The Master Plan of Evangelism* **and** *Ordering your Private World.*

Now that you comprehend how Paul shared his testimony, God wants to give you the wisdom and freedom to share your testimony with your small group. Remember what we have studied up to now:

(1) Keep it simple enough that a child can understand.

(2) Speak about your B.C. days, but not in too much detail.

(3) When you finish sharing your salvation experience, everyone listening should know exactly how to accept Christ.

(4) Zero in on what Jesus has done in you since you came to know Him, but be very transparent and honest about some of the trials you have experienced as a believer. We don't want anyone to view the Christian life as all peaches and cream, with no bumps and bruises along the way. We do, however, want our listeners to realize that although God didn't promise a smooth road, He did promise to put springs in the wagon!

Condense your testimony to 30 minutes or less. I suggest that you write it on paper and then record yourself sharing it. By listening to the recording you can determine what needs to be added or deleted. If you are like me, you will not enjoy listening to yourself. If you can bear it, however, it will greatly impact the way you share your testimony. Keep practicing it until you are completely comfortable with your message.

During the next six weeks, one group member per week will share his or her testimony in your small-group setting. (Assuming your group contains six members or less.) Because these testimonies will be no longer than 30 minutes each, you will have ample time for prayer, as well as time to discuss the materials covered during the week. Your group members can determine the order in which these testimonies will be given. Of course, if your group contains fewer than six members, a testimony will not be shared each week. However, since you will read and study *The Master Plan of Evangelism* (by Robert Coleman) and *Ordering Your Private World* (by Gordan MacDonald) during this six-week period, along with your weekly Scripture assignments, you will have plenty to discuss. If for some reason you choose not to work through *The Master Plan of Evangelism* and *Ordering Your Private World,* your testimonies and the Scripture assignments should stimulate ample discussion. I highly recommend, however, that you purchase and study these two books if at all possible. They are resources that you should read periodically for the rest of your life. Trust me, the benefits you gain will far outweigh your investment costs.

First Day—*Memorize Romans 3:20*

1. Start reading *The Master Plan of Evangelism.* This book describes how Jesus discipled the twelve, so it houses much food for thought. The first time I read it I could hardly put it down. Don't skip the introduction. Also refer to the study guide in the back of the book. Record any new insights.

2. Read Matthew 14-15 and record new insights.

What you read in the Gospel of Matthew should go well with what you glean from *The Master Plan of Evangelism.* As you continue to read through Matthew, notice how Jesus loved and discipled the twelve. Write down any new prayer requests in your prayer journal each day this week. List all answered prayer.

Second Day

1. Read the Preface of *The Master and His Plan,* (pp. 11-19). Also read page 9 in the study guide located in the back of the book. Answer the questions under *Learning Procedures* and *Achievement Goals* (pp. 10-12). Record any new insights.

2. Read Matthew 16-18. Record any new insights.

Third Day—*Memorize Romans 1:16*

1. Read the chapter titled *Selection* (pp. 21-37), and read page 13 in the study guide. Answer the questions under *Learning Procedures* and *Achievement Goals* (pp. 14-16).

Record any new insights.

2. Read Matthew 19-20 and record new insights.

Fourth Day

1. Read the chapter titled *Association* (pp. 38-49), and read page 17 in the study guide. Answer the questions under *Learning Procedures* and *Achievement Goals* (pp. 18-19). Record any new insights.

2. Read Matthew 21-22 and record new insights.

Fifth Day—*Memorize Romans 1:17*

1. Read the chapter titled *Consecration* (pp. 50-60), and read page 20 in the study guide. Answer the questions under *Learning Procedures* and *Achievement Goals* (pp. 21-24). Record any new insights.

2. Read Matthew 23-24 and record new insights.

Sixth Day

1. Read the chapter titled *Impartation* (pp. 61-72), and read page 25 in the study guide. Answer the questions under *Learning Procedures* (p. 26). Record any new insights.

2. Read Matthew 25-26 and record new insights.

Seventh Day

1. Read the chapter titled *Demonstration* (pp. 73-81), and read page 29 in the study guide. Answer the questions under *Learning Procedures* (pp. 29-30). Record any new insights.

2. Read Matthew 27-28 and record new insights.

Learning to Share Your Testimony
(B)

B. Application Weeks (Sharing Your Testimony), *The Master Plan of Evangelism* **and** *Ordering Your Private World.*

First Day—*Memorize Romans 5:1*

1. Make sure that you are continuing to work on your testimony. This task is so very important!!

2. Read the chapter titled *Delegation* (pp. 82-93), and read page 33 in the study guide. Answer the questions under *Learning Procedures* (p. 34). Record any new insights.

3. Read Luke 1 and record any new insights in your notebook. Luke was a Gentile and one of Paul's traveling companions. He was with Paul during Paul's first (Colossians 4:14, Philemon 24) and second (2Timothy 4:11) imprisonments in Rome. Luke not only wrote the Gospel of Luke, but also the book of Acts. He was not one of the original twelve apostles. The Gospel of Luke will blend in well with what you are learning from *The Master Plan of Evangelism* and what you will learn from *Ordering Your Private World*. Write down any new prayer requests in your prayer journal each day this week. List all answered prayer.

Second Day

1. Read the chapter titled *Supervision* (pp. 94-101), and read page 37 in the study guide. Answer the questions under *Learning Procedures* (p. 38). Record any new insights.

2. Read Luke 2-3. Record any new insights.

Third Day—*Memorize John 13:34*

1. Read the chapter titled *Reproduction* (pp. 102-114), and read page 40 in the study guide. Answer the questions under *Learning Procedures* (p. 41). Record any new insights.

2. Read Luke 4-5 and record new insights.

Fourth Day

1. Read the _Epilogue, The Master and Your Plan_ (pp. 115-126). Read the introduction to Lesson 10 (p. 44), Lesson 11 (pp. 48-49), Lesson 12 (p. 52), and Lesson 13 (p. 56) in the study guide. If you have time to answer any of the questions under _Learning Procedures_ in any of these lessons, feel free to do so. Record any new insights.

2. Read Luke 6-7. Record any new insights.

Fifth Day—_Memorize John 13:35_

1. We will now start reading _Ordering Your Private World._ This book is a tremendous resource for the person who has trouble with time management. It should be a true pleasure to read. Read the _Preface_ (pp. 7-11) and record new insights.

2. Read Luke 8 and record new insights.

Sixth Day

1. Answer the questions in the study guide (pp. 182-184).

2. Read Luke 9. Record any new insights.

Seventh Day

1. Read Chapter 1, _The Sinkhole Syndrome_ (pp. 12-19). Record any new insights.

2. Read Luke 10-11. Record any new insights in your notebook.

Learning to Share Your Testimony
(B)

B. Application Weeks (Sharing Your Testimony), *The Master Plan of Evangelism* **and** *Ordering Your Private World.*

First Day—*Memorize Galatians 2:20*

1. How are you coming on your testimony? Make sure you are continuing to work on it if you have not yet completed it!!

2. Answer the questions on Chapter One in the study guide (pp. 185-186).

3. Read Luke 12. Record any new insights. Write down any new prayer requests in your prayer journal, each day this week. List all answered prayer.

Second Day

1. Read Chapter Two, *The View from the Bridge* (pp. 19-25). Record any new insights.

2. Read Luke 13-14 and record new insights.

Third Day—*Memorize 2Corinthians 5:17*

1. Answer the questions on Chapter Two in the study guide (pp. 187-188).

2. Read Luke 15-16. Record any new insights.

Fourth Day

1. Read Chapter Three, *Caught in a Golden Cage* (pp. 26-40). Record any new insights.

2. Read Luke 17-18. Record any new insights.

Fifth Day—*Memorize 2Corinthians 5:21*

1. Answer the questions on Chapter Three in the study guide (pp.189-192).

2. Read Luke 19-20. Record any new insights.

Sixth Day

1. Read Chapter Four, *The Tragic Tale of a Successful Bum* (pp. 41-49). Record any new insights.

2. Read Luke 21-22 and record new insights.

Seventh Day

1. Answer the questions on Chapter Four in the study guide (pp.193-195).

2. Read Luke 23-24. Record any new insights.

Learning to Share Your Testimony
(B)

B. Application Weeks (Sharing Your Testimony), *The Master Plan of Evangelism*
and *Ordering Your Private World.*

First Day—*Memorize 2Corinthians 3:18*

1. Are you enjoying the testimonies of your group members?

How is yours coming along?

You won't regret the time you are setting aside to work on it! I promise!

2. Read Chapter Five, *Living as a Called Person* (pp. 50-61). Record any new insights.

3. Read Mark 1-2. Now that you have read the Gospels of Matthew and Luke back-to-back, notice how much more you glean from the Gospel of Mark. Remember that Mark is John Mark, who, earlier in his walk with Christ deserted Paul and Barnabas on Paul's first missionary journey. He was not one of the twelve apostles. Record any new insights. Write down any new prayer requests in your prayer journal, each day this week. List all answered prayer.

Second Day

1. Answer the questions on Chapter Five in the study guide (pp.196-198).

2. Mark 3-4. Record any new insights.

Third Day—*Memorize Philippians 4:6*

1. Read Chapter 6, *Has Anyone Seen My Time? I've Misplaced It!* (pp. 62-72). Record any new insights.

2. Read Mark 5-6 and record new insights.

Fourth Day

1. Answer the questions on Chapter Six in the study guide (pp. 199-202).

2. Read Mark 7-8. Record any new insights.

Fifth Day—*Memorize Philippians 4:7*

1. Read Chapter Seven, *Recapturing My Time* (pp. 73-85). Record any new insights.

2. Read Mark 9-10. Record any new insights.

Sixth Day

1. Answer the questions on Chapter Seven in the study guide (pp. 203-206).

2. Read Mark 11-12. Record any new insights.

Seventh Day

1. Read Chapter Eight, *The Better Man Lost* (pp. 86-98). Record new insights.

2. Read Mark 13-14 and record new insights in your notebook.

Learning to Share Your Testimony
(B)

B. Application Weeks (Sharing Your Testimony), *The Master Plan of Evangelism* **and** *Ordering Your Private World.*

First Day—*Memorize Philippians 1:6*

1. If you have not yet done so, you should be close to putting the finishing touches on your testimony. Press on!

2. Answer the questions on Chapter Eight in the study guide (pp. 207-210).

3. Read Mark 15-16. Record any new insights. Write down any new prayer requests in your prayer journal, each day this week. List all answered prayer.

Second Day

1. Read Chapter Nine, *The Sadness of a Book Never Read* (pp. 99-112). Record any new insights.

2. Read 1 John 1-3. This book was written by the same John, the apostle, who wrote the Gospel of John, 2 John, 3 John, and Revelation. Record any new insights.

Third Day—*Memorize Philippians 2:3*

1. Answer the questions on Chapter Nine in the study guide (pp. 211-213). Record any new insights.

2. Read 1 John 4-5, 2 John, 3 John. Record any new insights.

Fourth Day

1. Read Chapter Ten, *Order in the Garden* (pp. 113-123). Record any new insights.

2. Read Revelation 1-2. As was stated earlier, John the apostle wrote Revelation. As you read through this book, digest what you can and leave the rest for later. Your understanding will expand as you mature in your walk with Christ. Record any new insights.

Fifth Day—*Memorize 2Timothy 2:1*

1. Answer the questions on Chapter Ten in the study guide (pp. 214-216).

2. Read Revelation 3-4. Record any new insights.

Sixth Day

1. Read Chapter 11, *No Outer Props Necessary* (pp. 124-136). Record any new insights.

2. Read Revelation 5-6. Record any new insights.

Seventh Day

1. Answer the questions on Chapter Eleven in the study guide (pp. 217-219).

2. Read Revelation 7-8. Remember to digest what you can and press on. Record any new insights.

Learning to Share Your Testimony
(B)

B. Application Weeks (Sharing Your Testimony), *The Master Plan of Evangelism* **and** *Ordering Your Private World.*

First Day—*Memorize 2Timothy 2:2*

1. You should have completed your testimony by now. Isn't it rewarding to have it so fresh on your mind?

What portion of your testimony was the most difficult to prepare, and why?

2. Read Chapter Twelve, *Everything Has to Be Entered* (pp. 137-142). Record any new insights.

3. Read Revelation 9-10. Record any new insights. Write down any new prayer requests in your prayer journal, each day this week. List all answered prayer.

Second Day

1. Answer the questions on Chapter Twelve in study guide (pp. 220-221).

2. Read Revelation 11-12. Record any new insights.

Third Day—*Memorize 2Timothy 2:3*

1. Read Chapter Thirteen, *Seeing Through Heaven's Eyes* (pp. 143-158). Record any new insights.

2. Read Revelation 13-14. Record any new insights.

Fourth Day

1. Answer the questions on Chapter Thirteen in the study guide (pp. 222-225).

2. Read Revelation 15-16. Record any new insights.

Fifth Day

1. Read Chapter Fourteen, *Rest Beyond Leisure* (pp. 159-175). Record any new insights.

2. Read Revelation 17-18 and record new insights. Digest what you can and read on!

Sixth Day

1. Answer the questions on Chapter Fourteen (pp. 226-228).

2. Read Revelation 19-20. Record any new insights.

Seventh Day

1. Read the Epilogue, *The Spinning Wheel* (pp. 176-181). Record any new insights.

2. Read Revelation 21-22 and record new insights.

Learning to Share Your Testimony
(C)

First Day—*Memorize Titus 3:5*
1. When you were preparing your testimony, what was your greatest fear?

What was the most encouraging thing that happened?

How did you feel as you presented your testimony to the group? (Feel free to be open here.)

2. Now that you have given your testimony, will you feel more comfortable sharing it with others?

Do you think you could present it before a much larger group?

Why or why not?

What was the most important thing you learned as your group members shared their testimonies? Be specific.

What has this section of the course done to draw you closer to your group members?

3. Read Psalm 119:1-32 and write down new insights that relate to spending time in God's Word. Write down any new prayer requests in your prayer journal, each day this

week. Also list all answered prayer.

Second Day

1. Why should we feel free to share our salvation experience without fear?

Validate your answer with Scripture.

List at least three instances in God's Word where individuals speak boldly of our Lord in the midst of intense persecution. (You may answer this question by using either Old or New Testament Scripture.)

2. Read Daniel chapters one and three to receive encouragement to stand in boldness. What impressed you the most in these two chapters?

3. Read Psalm 119:33-64 and write down new insights that relate to spending time in God's Word.

Third Day

1. Read 2Timothy 1:1-18. 2Timothy 1:7 says, *"For God has not given us a spirit of timidity."* (Timidity here means fear.) What does this sentence say to you?

Who wrote these words to Timothy?

From where did he write it?

Was the man who wrote this line "timid" when it came to sharing his faith in Christ?

Give at least three examples from Scripture that support your answer.

2. Read Psalm 119:65-96 and write down new insights that relate to spending time in God's Word.

Fourth Day

1. Under what circumstances do you find it the most difficult to share your faith?

Must you always share your faith verbally for others to see Jesus in your life? Explain.

When were you last used by the Lord to share your faith without saying a word?

Try to think of some examples in Scripture where God used an individual without that person ever speaking.

2. What person has inspired you the most in your walk with Christ? What did you see in his/her life that drew you to that individual?

Could you drop that person a note to express your appreciation for what he/she has meant to you?

3. Read Psalm 119:97-128 and write down new insights that relate to spending time in God's Word.

Fifth Day

1. In 2Timothy 1:7 what does "power" mean?

From where does it come?

How do we continue in it?

How does this principal tie in with Paul's words in 1Thessalonians 1:5?

Do you desire to have power in your Christian experience?

If you have it, how did you obtain it?

If you don't have it, what needs to take place before you can experience it?

2. What does "love" mean in 2Timothy 1:7?

Where does this love originate?

How do we continue in it?

Do you consider yourself capable of loving others with unconditional love?

If not, what is hindering you from doing so?

How do you respond to unconditional love?

3. Read Psalm 119:129-160 and write down new insights that relate to spending time in God's Word.

Sixth Day

1. What does "discipline" mean in 2Timothy 1:7?

How do we attain this discipline?

What must we do to continue in it?

2. Is it important for people to know that you love and care for them?

If so, how can you best convey this love as you share your faith?

3. Read this week's lesson and record new insights.

4. Read Psalm 119:161-176 and write down new insights that relate to spending time in God's Word.

Learning to Share Your Testimony
(C)

C. Why You Can Share your Testimony without Fear

This lesson will cover 2Timothy 1:7, which says, *"For God has not given us a spirit of timidity, but of power and love and discipline."* God has not given us a spirit of timidity (or fear), but one of power and love and discipline (or sound judgment). The word timidity comes from the Greek word "deilia," which refers to a "cowardly" frame of mind. Paul wanted Timothy to realize that he did not have to act in a cowardly manner while exercising his spiritual gift (2Timothy 1:6-7).

This truth applies to us as well. We never have to respond in a cowardly manner, regardless of our circumstance. We are free to let the Lord speak through us in any situation, but we must make sure that the Lord speaks and not us. This last statement deserves much attention, especially for those who might be beginning their walk with Christ. Let's examine it more closely.

I will never forget the first time I read 2Timothy 1:7. What an experience! Although I was a "babe" in Christ, I was highly motivated to share what He had done for me. However, when I read 2Timothy 1:7, I only digested the first part of the verse: *"For God has not given us a spirit of timidity..."* This news was so terrific that I completely overlooked what followed: *"... but of power and love and discipline."* I lacked the maturity to realize the danger of taking Scripture out of context, so I went on my merry way, in my own strength, trying to do God's work "for" Him. After all, I no longer had to act like a coward. The Word of God said so, and I could "stand" on it. So "stand" I did! I had much labor but little fruit. Consequently, the Lord used hardship to force me to consider the remaining portion of the verse, *"...but of power and love and discipline."* "Power" is from the Greek word "dunamis," meaning "energy." I soon learned that it takes more than words expressed in the form of information to change someone's heart. Our society is saturated with raw information, but only one source, God Himself, transforms information into revelation. Only revealed truth can change lives. (Revealed truth allows a person to understand how the information applies to his everyday walk with Christ.)

Before we can share our salvation experience with power, we must see that God alone adds strength and meaning to what we have to say. The power comes from Him as we learn to walk intimately with our Creator and begin to view life from His perspective.

In 1Thessalonians 1:5 Paul states that his preaching came not only in word (information) but also in power (from the same root word used for power in 2Timothy 1:7). The word "power" can be interpreted as "effectiveness" in this case.

Thus, Paul's words contained more than raw information. When we, like Paul, walk in intimacy with Christ, we will stand amazed as God adds effectiveness to our message. But "effectiveness" only results as we yield to His life within us. We then learn to "rest" (Hebrews 4:9) as He expresses His awesome character through our unique personalities. All power comes from Him as we yield to Him (Galatians 2:20, John 15:5).

As we walk in fellowship with Christ, the fruit of the Spirit is manifested through us to others. Paul states in Galatians 5:22 that the first fruit of the Spirit is love. The Greek word for this type of love is "agape," which is the same word used for love in 2Timothy 1:7. Agape love is unconditional love, a love that says, "I love you regardless." It says, "Do anything you like, but when the dust settles, my love will remain."

If we learn to walk in the Spirit (which simply means to walk in fellowship with Christ), agape love will flow through our lives to others. Then God's love and sensitivity will be manifested to those around us. God's kindness leads us to repentance (Romans 2:4), and this same kindness will lead others to repentance.

Above all else, we must never use truth as a battering ram. The following quote, the source of which is unknown to me, applies here: Truth without love is brutality, but love without truth is hypocrisy." Think about what this says. Truth without love is brutal—BRUTAL!

I realize that we will be persecuted when we teach truth, but let's make sure we are persecuted for what the Word of God says and not for our lack of compassion for others. I have watched Christians express truth without love, reap rejection, and mistakenly believe they are truly suffering for the cause of Christ. They act almost prideful about the degree to which they are being persecuted. Some even go so far as to measure their spirituality by the amount of persecution they endure. This measurement is false and should be avoided at all costs. The true measure of spiritual maturity is based on how much of Galatians 5:22-23 others see in the believer's life. If this fruit is manifested, it will have an awesome impact on everyone around. The fruit will bring true persecution from those who do not know Christ, but it will encourage those who do. Remember Stephen!

The word "discipline" in 2Timothy 1:7 (the King James Version uses "sound mind") also means, "a calm but energetic state of mind," or "self-control." We learn to manifest self-control, a fruit of the Spirit, as we write the Word of God on our minds. Then, through the help of the Holy Spirit, we apply God's Word to every situation in our lives. Much time is required in learning to walk in the Spirit and self-control, so the believer should not become overly discouraged.

Even Paul struggled in this area, but victory was finally achieved after several years of sitting alone with his God. Because no two people are alike, we must constantly yield to the Spirit when sharing our lives with others. Sometimes we speak boldly. At other times we say nothing at all. The goal is to become all things to all people (1Corinthians 9:22).

We have learned:

1. We have no cause for fear! We should never feel cowardly when sharing what Christ has done in us. Whatever we share must be done by trusting Christ to do it through us.

2. The power (effectiveness) in our message comes from Christ. If we walk in close fellowship with Him, we are filled with God's Spirit, and true power (effectiveness) is bound to show within our message. If we look to ourselves for this power and effectiveness, we will have much information and activity, but no lasting fruit.

3. We must speak the truth in love. This message will occur only if we trust Christ to speak through us. The first fruit of the Spirit (love) will then be radiated from our message, which will captivate the attention of all who listen. Because Jesus knew how to love unconditionally, multitudes of people followed Him. His listeners knew that He cared for their wellbeing, but He loved them enough to teach them truth without compromise. Consequently, many forsook and persecuted Him. We can expect the same result but we can rest assured that what we speak in "agape" love will never be forgotten. Love changes lives and never fails (1Corinthians 13:8).

4. We must exercise self-control and yield to the Holy Spirit; we must learn to be all things to all people. Almost everyone we meet will have a different set of needs, so we should respond differently to each individual. God's Spirit will teach us more about doing so as we mature in the faith. God can then use us to minister to a variety of needs in the lives of others.

"Now to Him who is able to do exceedingly abundantly beyond all that we ask or think, according to the power that works within us..." Spoken by a man who knew this to be absolute truth: Paul the Apostle, whose goal, ambition, aspiration, aim, and objective was not activity, but intimacy with the Holy Son of God.

Have you started praying for someone to pour your life into? If so, you won't be sorry.

May our Lord bless you and meet your every need. Stay in the Book and on your knees, and all will be well.

Thanks again for giving us this time with you. It truly blesses us to know that you have been in the Word these past 19 weeks. You will see God do great things with the truth He has written on your heart (mind). Walk on! Jesus is on His throne and all is well.

Memory Verses

Go therefore and make disciples of all the nations, baptizing them in the name of the Father and the Son and the Holy Spirit, 20 teaching them to observe all that I commanded you; and lo, I am with you always, even to the end of the age. (Matthew 28:19-20)

No one can serve two masters; for either he will hate the one and love the other, or he will be devoted to one and despise the other. You cannot serve God and wealth. (Matthew 6:24)

But seek first His kingdom and His righteousness, and all these things will be added to you. (Matthew 6:33)

For we have brought nothing into the world, so we cannot take anything out of it either. (1Timothy 6:7)

If we have food and covering, with these we shall be content. (1Timothy 6:8)

He who has found his life will lose it, and he who has lost his life for My sake will find it. (Matthew 10:39)

But whatever things were gain to me, those things I have counted as loss for the sake of Christ. (Philippians 3:7)

More than that, I count all things to be loss in view of the surpassing value of knowing Christ Jesus my Lord, for whom I have suffered the loss of all things, and count them but rubbish so that I may gain Christ, (Philippians 3:8)

Indeed, all who desire to live godly in Christ Jesus will be persecuted. (2Timothy 3:12)

And do not get drunk with wine, for that is dissipation, but be filled with the Spirit, (Ephesians 5:18)

So Jesus was saying to those Jews who had believed Him, "If you continue in My word, then you are truly disciples of Mine; and you will know the truth, and the truth will make you free." (John 8:31-32)

But as many as received Him, to them He gave the right to become children of God, even to those who believe in His name, (John 1:12)

Jesus said to him, "I am the way, and the truth, and the life; no one comes to the Father but through Me." (John 14:6)

For by grace you have been saved through faith; and that not of yourselves, it is the gift of God; not as a result of works, so that no one may boast. (Ephesians 2:8-9)

For He rescued us from the domain of darkness, and transferred us to the kingdom of His beloved Son, (Colossians 1:13)

Therefore there is now no condemnation for those who are in Christ Jesus. (Romans 8:1)

Now to Him who is able to keep you from stumbling, and to make you stand in the presence of His glory blameless with great joy, (Jude 24)

For by one offering He has perfected for all time those who are sanctified. (Hebrews 10:14)

So there remains a Sabbath rest for the people of God. (Hebrews 4:9)

For the one who has entered His rest has himself also rested from his works, as God did from His. (Hebrews 4:10)

For the word of God is living and active and sharper than any two-edged sword, and piercing as far as the division of soul and spirit, of both joints and marrow, and able to judge the thoughts and intentions of the heart. (Hebrews 4:12)

Therefore let us draw near with confidence to the throne of grace, so that we may receive mercy and find grace to help in time of need. (Hebrews 4:16)

Be kind to one another, tender-hearted, forgiving each other, just as God in Christ also has forgiven you. (Ephesians 4:32)

When you were dead in your transgressions and the uncircumcision of your flesh, He made you alive together with Him, having forgiven us all our transgressions, (Colossians 2:13)

Now may the God of peace Himself sanctify you entirely; and may your spirit and soul and body be preserved complete, without blame at the coming of our Lord Jesus Christ. (1 Thessalonians 5:23)

So faith comes from hearing, and hearing by the word of Christ. (Romans 10:17)

"And there is salvation in no one else; for there is no other name under heaven that has been given among men by which we must be saved." (Acts 4:12)

because by the works of the Law no flesh will be justified in His sight; for through the Law comes the knowledge of sin. (Romans 3:20)

For I am not ashamed of the gospel, for it is the power of God for salvation to everyone who believes, to the Jew first and also to the Greek. (Romans 1:16)

For in it the righteousness of God is revealed from faith to faith; as it is written, "BUT THE RIGHTEOUS man SHALL LIVE BY FAITH." (Romans 1:17)

Therefore, having been justified by faith, we have peace with God through our Lord Jesus Christ, (Romans 5:1)

A new commandment I give to you, that you love one another, even as I have loved you, that you also love one another. (John 13:34)

By this all men will know that you are My disciples, if you have love for one another. (John 13:35)

I have been crucified with Christ; and it is no longer I who live, but Christ lives in me; and the life which I now live in the flesh I live by faith in the Son of God, who loved me and gave Himself up for me. (Galatians 2:20)

Therefore if anyone is in Christ, he is a new creature; the old things passed away; behold, new things have come. (2Corinthians 5:17)

He made Him who knew no sin to be sin on our behalf, so that we might become the righteousness of God in Him. (2Corinthians 5:21)

But we all, with unveiled face, beholding as in a mirror the glory of the Lord, are being transformed into the same image from glory to glory, just as from the Lord, the Spirit. (2Corinthians 3:18)

Be anxious for nothing, but in everything by prayer and supplication with thanksgiving let your requests be made known to God. (Philippians 4:6)
And the peace of God, which surpasses all comprehension, will guard your hearts and your minds in Christ Jesus. (Philippians 4:7)

For I am confident of this very thing, that He who began a good work in you will perfect it until the day of Christ Jesus.   (Philippians 1:6)

Do nothing from selfishness or empty conceit, but with humility of mind regard one another as more important than yourselves; (Philippians 2:3)

You therefore, my son, be strong in the grace that is in Christ Jesus. (2Timothy 2:1)

The things which you have heard from me in the presence of many witnesses, entrust these to faithful men who will be able to teach others also. (2Timothy 2:2)

Suffer hardship with me, as a good soldier of Christ Jesus. (2Timothy 2:3)

He saved us, not on the basis of deeds which we have done in righteousness, but according to His mercy, by the washing of regeneration and renewing by the Holy Spirit, (Titus 3:5)

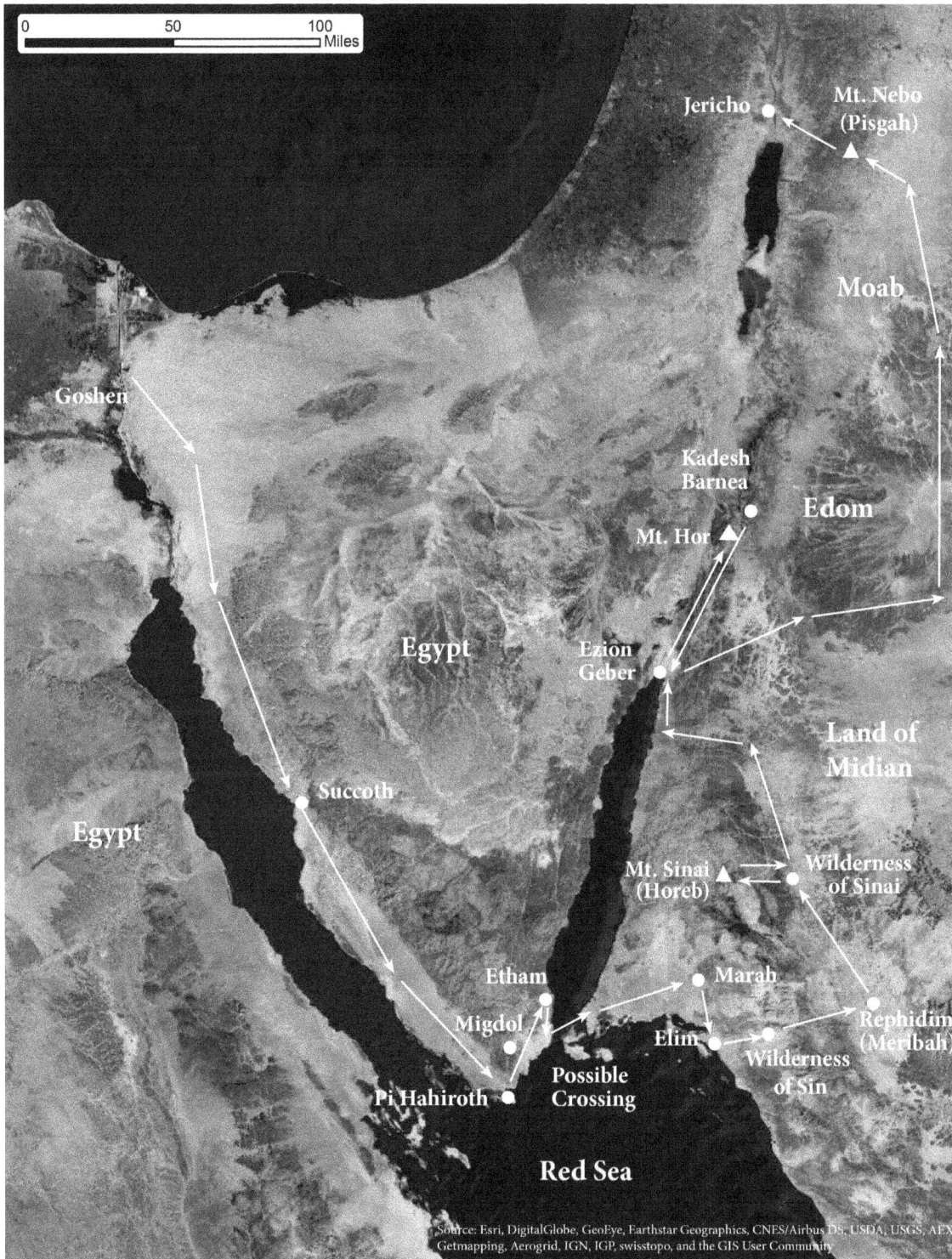

Map Section

From Egypt To Canaan

0   50   100
Miles

Jericho   Mt. Nebo (Pisgah)

Moab

Goshen

Kadesh Barnea

Mt. Hor   Edom

Egypt

Ezion Geber

Land of Midian

Egypt

Succoth

Mt. Sinai (Horeb)   Wilderness of Sinai

Etham   Marah

Migdol   Rephidim (Meribah)

Elim

Pi Hahiroth   Possible Crossing   Wilderness of Sin

Red Sea

Source: Esri, DigitalGlobe, GeoEye, Earthstar Geographics, CNES/Airbus DS, USDA, USGS, AEX
Getmapping, Aerogrid, IGN, IGP, swisstopo, and the GIS User Community

Journeys of Paul's Early Life

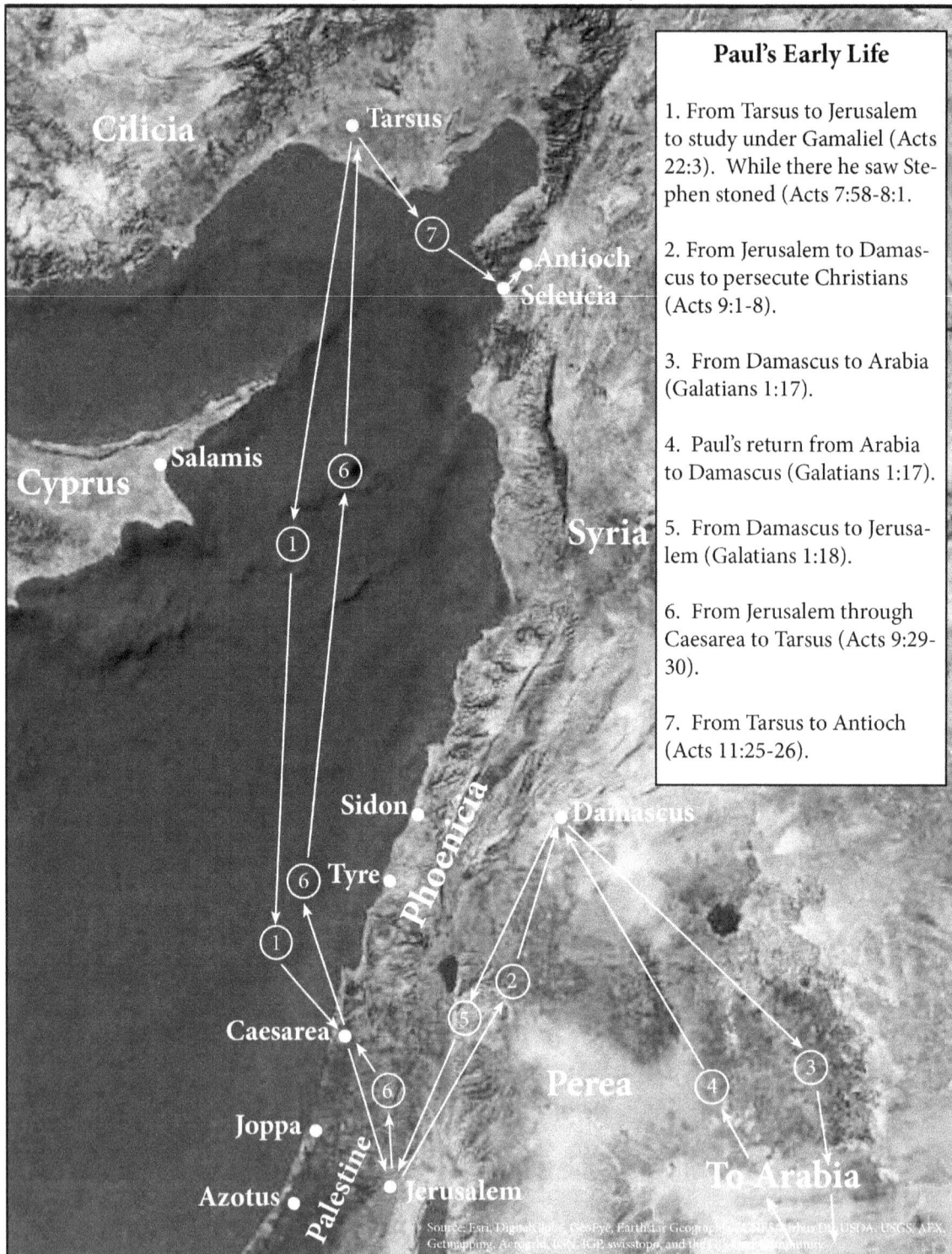

Paul's Early Life

1. From Tarsus to Jerusalem to study under Gamaliel (Acts 22:3). While there he saw Stephen stoned (Acts 7:58-8:1.

2. From Jerusalem to Damascus to persecute Christians (Acts 9:1-8).

3. From Damascus to Arabia (Galatians 1:17).

4. Paul's return from Arabia to Damascus (Galatians 1:17).

5. From Damascus to Jerusalem (Galatians 1:18).

6. From Jerusalem through Caesarea to Tarsus (Acts 9:29-30).

7. From Tarsus to Antioch (Acts 11:25-26).

Paul's First Missionary Journey

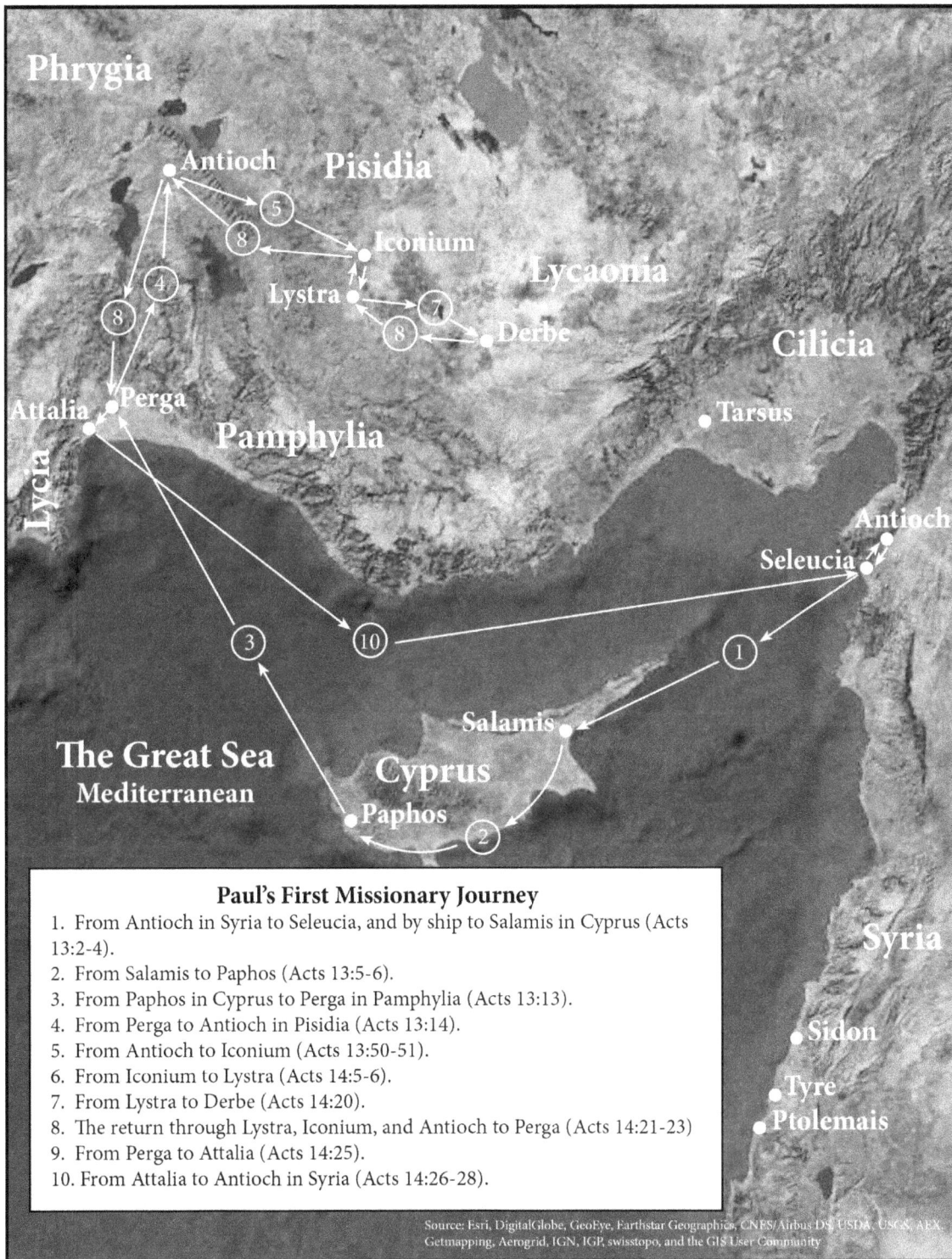

Paul's First Missionary Journey

1. From Antioch in Syria to Seleucia, and by ship to Salamis in Cyprus (Acts 13:2-4).
2. From Salamis to Paphos (Acts 13:5-6).
3. From Paphos in Cyprus to Perga in Pamphylia (Acts 13:13).
4. From Perga to Antioch in Pisidia (Acts 13:14).
5. From Antioch to Iconium (Acts 13:50-51).
6. From Iconium to Lystra (Acts 14:5-6).
7. From Lystra to Derbe (Acts 14:20).
8. The return through Lystra, Iconium, and Antioch to Perga (Acts 14:21-23)
9. From Perga to Attalia (Acts 14:25).
10. From Attalia to Antioch in Syria (Acts 14:26-28).

Source: Esri, DigitalGlobe, GeoEye, Earthstar Geographics, CNES/Airbus DS, USDA, USGS, AEX, Getmapping, Aerogrid, IGN, IGP, swisstopo, and the GIS User Community

Paul's Second Missionary Journey

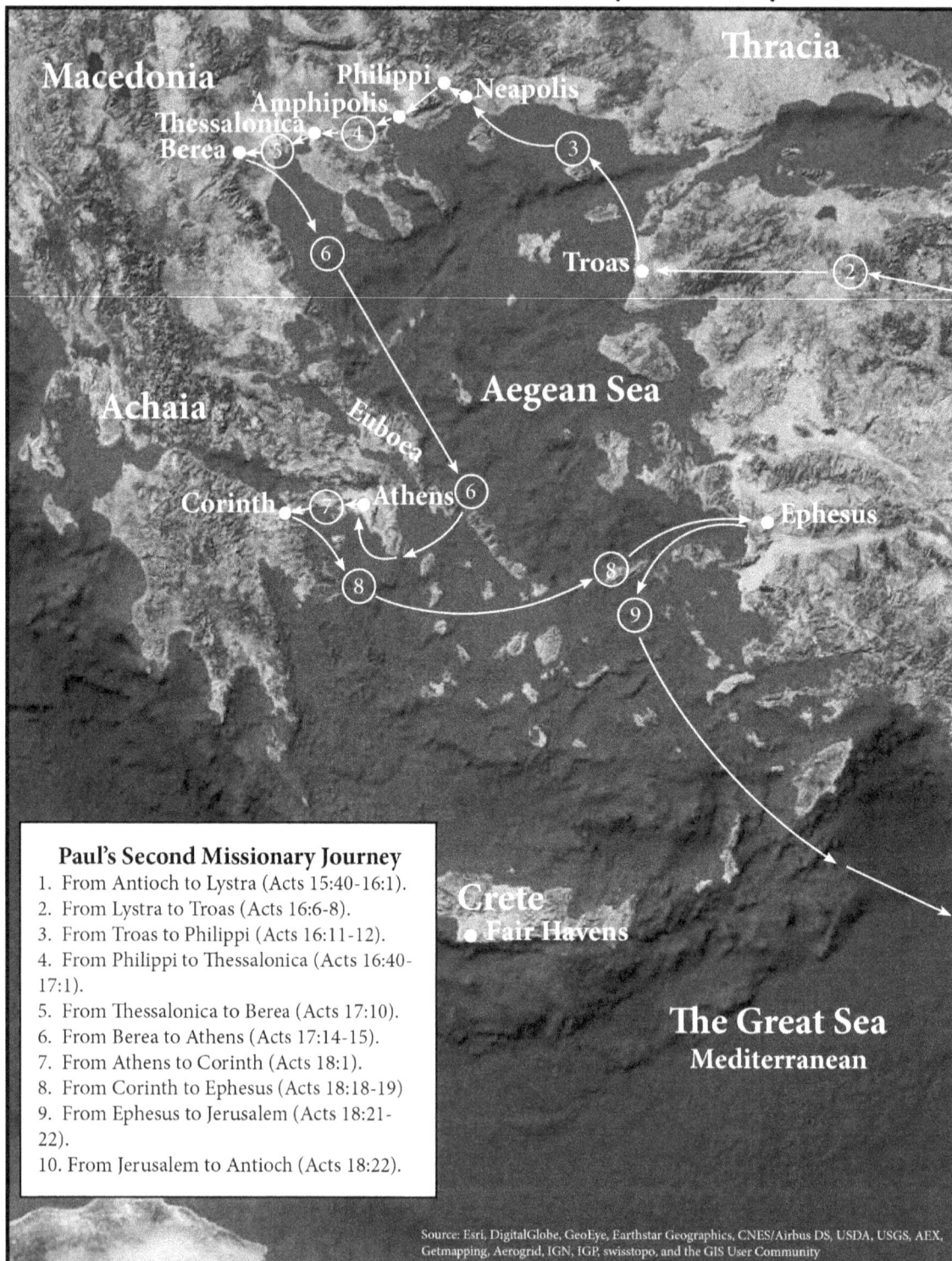

Paul's Second Missionary Journey
1. From Antioch to Lystra (Acts 15:40-16:1).
2. From Lystra to Troas (Acts 16:6-8).
3. From Troas to Philippi (Acts 16:11-12).
4. From Philippi to Thessalonica (Acts 16:40-17:1).
5. From Thessalonica to Berea (Acts 17:10).
6. From Berea to Athens (Acts 17:14-15).
7. From Athens to Corinth (Acts 18:1).
8. From Corinth to Ephesus (Acts 18:18-19)
9. From Ephesus to Jerusalem (Acts 18:21-22).
10. From Jerusalem to Antioch (Acts 18:22).

Source: Esri, DigitalGlobe, GeoEye, Earthstar Geographics, CNES/Airbus DS, USDA, USGS, AEX, Getmapping, Aerogrid, IGN, IGP, swisstopo, and the GIS User Community

Paul's Second Missionary Journey

Paul's Third Missionary Journey

Paul's Third Missionary Journey

1. From Antioch in Syria to Galatia (Acts 18:22-23).
2. From Galatia through Phrygia to Ephesus (Acts 19:1).
3. From Ephesus through Macedonia to Corinth (Acts 20:1-2).
4. From Corinth through Macedonia to Troas (Acts 20:3-6).
5. From Troas to Assos, then by sea to Miletus (Acts 20:13-15).
6. From Miletus through Rhodes and Patara to Tyre (Acts 21:1-3).
7. From Tyre through Caesarea to Jerusalem (Acts 21:7-15).

Source: Esri, DigitalGlobe, GeoEye, Earthstar Geographics, CNES/Airbus DS, USDA, USGS, AEX, Getmapping, Aerogrid, IGN, IGP, swisstopo, and the GIS User Community

Paul's Third Missionary Journey

Bithynia

Mysia

Galatia

Lydia ②

Phrygia

Asia

Antioch ②

Pisidia   Iconium

Colossae   Lystra

Lycaonia

Cilicia

Derbe ①

Pamphylia   Tarsus ①

Lycia

Antioch

Rhodes   Patara

Seleucia

Salamis

Cyprus

Paphos

Syria

Sidon

The Great Sea ⑥   Tyre

Mediterranean   ⑦ Ptolemais

Caesarea

Jerusalem

Paul's Voyage to Rome

Paul's Voyage to Rome